W9-AAT-144

GETTING
RADIO
AIRPLAY

GETTING RADIO AIRPLAY

FIRST EDITION

WRITTEN AND EDITED BY

GARY HUSTWIT

ROCKPRESS PUBLISHING

P.O. BOX 99090 SAN DIEGO CA 92169 USA

© 1992 Rockpress Publishing Company.
All rights reserved. No part of this publication may be reproduced, stored
in a retrieval system or transmitted, in any form or by any means,
electronic, mechanical, photocopying, recording or otherwise, without the
prior written permission of the copyright holder.

This publication is designed to provide accurate and authoritative
information in regard to the subject matter covered. Every effort has been
made to provide correct information, however, the publisher does not
guarantee the accuracy of, or assume responsibility for, information
included in or omitted from this publication. Listings in this book do not
constitute an endorsement or recommendation from the publisher.

This book was created on an Apple Macintosh Classic computer using
Microsoft Word and Aldus PageMaker, output to an Apple Personal
LaserWriter LS printer.

Cover design by Jennifer Gulledge.

Thanks Mom, Sharon, Valerie, Michelle, Janyce, World Library,
Rockpress, and all the people who were interviewed for this book.

Thanks also to Brad Smith, Todd Souvignier and everyone at Mix
Bookshelf.

Special thanks to William A. Hustwit and especially Denise Therieau.

ISBN 0-9627013-1-9
Library of Congress Catalog Card No. 91-068143

Printed in the United States of America.

Contents

Introduction

Getting exposure for their music is perhaps the hardest task emerging musicians face. With the major corporate record labels spending millions of dollars annually to catch the eye of radio staff, press and retailers; thousands of independent artists get overlooked. Music that is just as good as (usually better than) the major label releases will usually go unnoticed unless the artist has the resources and desire to expose his or her music.

How can you compete with the multi-million dollar ad budgets and huge promotional staffs of the big record labels? Well, you can't. You *can* increase the odds of your music getting heard, however. The people interviewed in this book can provide you with tips and insight into what it takes to get your music noticed. In this book, I've concentrated on how to get radio airplay for your independently released music. You'll find that in most of the interviews, we usually stray off course and include thoughts and opinions on the entire experience of releasing your own music. I've tried to talk with people from both sides of the issue; from the record label or artists' point of view and from the radio station personnel's point of view. Hopefully, through their observations, you'll be able to better understand the state of radio in the 1990s.

I've combined these interviews with a directory of 900 college, public and commercial radio stations, information on what to send to these stations and how to get them to play your release. I'll also cover the radio trade publications and how they can help you, and I'll hopefully answer any questions you may have concerning what format to send (LP, cassette, CD) or other topics concerning radio in general.

First of all, you have to realize how many records get sent to each individual radio station every week: literally hundreds. Your ability to stand out from the rest of the heap will directly affect your chances of getting played. Whether it's your name, your packaging, ads you've taken out or other exposure you've gotten; there *has* to be some reason for the music director to listen to your record. The vast majority of independent artists will have to start out with college and public stations, and after they've proved themselves there move on to commercial radio.

Unfortunately, there is usually a direct correlation between the amount of money spent (on ads, phone calls to the stations, postage, etc.) and the amount of airplay received. This doesn't mean you have to have money to burn in order to get your music exposed on radio, but it sure helps. This book was published to help musicians with limited resources get radio airplay. Getting even a little airplay on college or public radio stations can help you book a tour, sell records, gain fans and attract the attention of larger record labels, if that's your goal. Whatever your reasons are for wanting radio airplay, the information in this book will definitely help you. Best wishes and good luck!

- Gary Hustwit

Radio Overview

There are three types of radio stations that we'll be discussing in this book: commercial, college and public. Commercial stations sell advertising and usually play one format or style of music exclusively. College and public stations don't sell ads. Frequently businesses sponsor shows by making a donation to the college or the stations have fundraising drives. The majority of college and public stations play many different types of music during the course of a day. They have specialty shows that feature everything from hardcore punk to jazz to folk.

For the independent artist, like yourself, who is releasing his or her own music or the music of a band, the best chance you have of getting your music played on radio is with the college and public stations. First of all, these stations don't sell advertising. When a commercial station is selling ads, a bigger audience share and higher ratings allow it to charge more for its advertising. This need for higher listenership and profits means that commercial stations will play what they feel are the most popular, safe songs of whatever musical style they program. They don't want to scare away listeners with new, unproven artists that the listeners aren't familiar with. With a few exceptions, only when new artists have been proven in the college / public radio arena, or there is a huge promotional campaign behind those new artists, will commercial stations add them to their playlist.

College and public stations, on the other hand, are non-profit and don't need ratings or listener share to sell ads. They are free to play whatever music they like, and the majority do not have a rigid playlist; the DJs can play whatever they want during their shows. College and public radio are probably the last re-maining media where new and unproven musicians have a chance of getting played. There are hundreds of these stations across the country, and the people at these stations are looking for new music. It's up to independent artists like yourself to get it out to them. The keys to getting your music played are to identify which stations will most likely play your music, to manufacture your release in a format that can be played by today's radio stations, and to get the attention of the Music Directors at the stations.

If you can get your music played on college and public stations, you'll have a much better chance of then receiving commercial radio airplay. Playlists with your name on them, from *any* radio station, are a good addition to your press kit. Another factor is the amount of money being spent by the major labels to get commercial stations to play their releases; in ads, daily phone calls, expensive promotions, etc. It's easier for an emerging artist to get the attention of college and public stations. So, throughout this book, we'll concentrate first on attacking the college and public stations, and let commercial fall in behind them.

Radio Terminology

The following is a small list of radio terms that you'll need to know in order to communicate with radio station personnel and others in the trade.

Add - The act of adding a new song to the station's playlist.

Cart - A tape system, similar to an 8-track tape but with only one, endless track. Designed for easy cueing. Frequently used for station IDs, public service announcements, commercials and frequently played songs.

Cue (or cue up) - To find the beginning of a certain song in order to play it.

Format - The style of music that a station plays. Also refers to recording media (LP, cassette, CD).

MD - Music Director. The person at the station who listens to, or auditions, new music sent to the station and decides which new records the station will play.

Mersh - Slang for commercial, or commercial sounding music.

PD - Program Director. The person who decides when and how often a certain song is played. The MD and PD usually work together to determine the station's playlist.

Playlist - A list of the songs a station plays, or has played during a given week or month. This is broken down into categories, called rotations, that represent how often a particular song was played: Heavy, medium and light rotation. A playlist also lists what new songs were added during that period.

Promo - Short for promotions or promotional. Used to designate the person from a record label who calls stations trying to get that label's music played (see *shmoozing*), and any materials or records that get sent to the stations.

Segue - (segg´-way) The time betwwen the end of one song and the beginning of the next.

Shmooze - The act (or art) of meeting and talking to people in the music industry, and getting them to do what you want them to do. (play / buy your record, etc.)

Track - (or **cut**) A song or piece of music. **Tracking** refers to keeping track of when and where your record is being played.

Trades - Radio industry trade publications. (See **Trade Publications** chapter)

Besides the standard genres (metal, jazz, rap (urban) etc.) these abbreviations are sometimes used when discussing radio formats:

AOR - Album Oriented Rock **CHR** - Contemporary Hit Radio
AC - Adult Contemporary **NAC** - New Adult Cont. (New Age)

These are only a few of the terms used in radio today; you'll learn more by reading the trades and talking to the people at the stations. Also, during this book, the word "record" will sometimes be used to designate all recording formats; vinyl, tape, compact disc, etc.

A Quick Outline

Here's a brief outline of the steps you'll need to take in order to get your music played on radio, assuming you already have your finished recording. For more information on each step, read the appropriate chapter.

1. Get sample copies of the trade publications.

2. Identify which stations are most likely to play your music. Compare your style to the artists listed in each station's playlist.

3. Send review copies to the trades.

4. Make follow-up calls to the trades to make sure they received your material and to see if they're going to review it.

5. Take out advertisements in the trades.* Time them to come out the week your records reach the stations.

6. Send records to the stations. The number you send depends on your budget and your ability to follow-up on the send-out.

7. Make follow-up phone calls to the stations to make sure they received your record and to see if they've listened to it, added it to their playlist, hate it, etc.

* This is optional and depends on your budget. For more information on trade publication ads and their effectiveness, read the **Trade Publications** and **Interviews** sections.

By following these steps, you'll maximize your chances of getting your music played on radio. This is a general outline that applies to all styles of music. The methods in this book will not guarantee that you receive airplay; they are designed to steer you through the proper channels to give your independent release the most exposure possible. Your level of success depends on how committed you are to getting your music heard. It's a serious investment of both time and money, but the bottom line is that the *music* has to be there. Plain and simple; if your music isn't any good, no one's going to play it. If you believe in your music, be persistent and enthusiastic about it. Hopefully this will rub off on the right people.

Format Selection

The format (vinyl, cassette, CD) on which you send your music to radio stations plays a huge part in determining whether or not it will get played. Your options concerning format really depend on your budget and whether or not you can afford to press different formats for radio and retail.

Before you press your release, make sure your recording quality is the best it can be, or at least the best you can afford. Poor recording quality will stop your release from even being considered for airplay.

With a few exceptions (local music shows being one of them), most radio stations will not play cassettes from unknown artists. It's too hard to isolate individual songs, and the DJs don't have the time to fast forward and rewind all over the tape looking for a particular cut. Radio stations are set up to play vinyl records and, nowadays, almost exclusively CDs.

Vinyl

"Vinyl? Isn't that a dead format?" you ask. Depending on your style of music, it *may* be as far as retail is concerned, but radio stations, especially college and public stations, still rely on vinyl, both 12" and 7". The majority of these stations have CD players, too, but they probably have a huge collection of vinyl that is still played every day. So for most of you, I'd recommend either 12" or 7" vinyl or a compact disc, either full length or CD5 single. You may consider pressing vinyl for radio and CD's for retail and press, but in today's music industry you probably can't go wrong pressing only CDs.

CD5 Singles

If you have the money, CD5 singles are definitely a good bet for radio. A typical major label or large independent label would send a CD5 single in a clear jewel box with no insert or sleeve; all the information is on the actual disc. Whatever your record packaging looks like, it has to look professional, but if the radio version that you're sending is different than your retail packaging, make the radio version as utilitarian as possible. Don't spend a fortune on full-color packaging if the product is only going to be sent to radio. Spend your money on the *recording*.

Cassettes

I strongly suggest that you do not send cassettes to radio stations. If you *have* to send cassettes due to budget constraints, send a cassette single, with one song on each side. It's easier to play, and therefore has a better chance of actually being played (although not much). My advice is to save your money and put out a more radio-friendly format. As you will read in the **Interviews** section, most Music Directors will not even *listen* to a cassette. If you *do* make cassettes, though, don't knock yourself out making a full-color printed J-card; once again, go for the stripped-down, inter-industry look.

If you know someone who works at a radio station (or even if you don't) go in and try to take a look at what other bands and labels are sending. You may get some ideas for packaging your release for radio.

Format	For radio?	For retail?
7" vinyl	maybe*	maybe**
12" vinyl	maybe*	maybe**
Cassette single	no***	yes
Full length cassettte	no	yes
CD5 single	yes	yes
Full length CD	yes	yes

* Most stations still play vinyl, but the majority of new releases sent to radio stations are on CD.
** Alternative rock, hardcore, rap, dance music: yes. All others: no.
*** Unless it's all you can afford. It'd be better to save up your money and use another format.

There's more information about formats and what radio station Music Directors want to receive in the **Interviews** section.

ATLANTIC RECORDING CORPORATION
75 ROCKEFELLER PLAZA, NEW YORK, N.Y. 10019
TELEPHONE: (212) 484-6000
CABLE ADDRESS: ATCOMUSIC
TWX 420275

September 22, 1988

Motherwit Records
P.O. Box 9666
San Diego, CA 92109

Dear Label Manager:

I am an A & R Research Assistant in the alternative
music department at Atlantic. Glenn, the music director
at WXYC in Chapel Hill, NC suggested that we give a listen
to The Charms. I would greatly appreciate receiving a
copy if possible.

Thank you in advance.

Regards,

Evon Handras
A & R Research Assistant

Above: The major labels listen to college radio, too.

The Send-out

So you've got a record and you want to send it to radio. What should you include with that record? How should it be packaged? Who should it be addressed to? Where do you send it? We'll start with the question of which stations you should send records.

Where To Send Them

In your local area, you probably know which stations will potentially play your record. If you're going to place advertisements in the national radio trade publications, you can send records to stations all over the country. Unless you are going to put an ad in the trades, or have some other type of national exposure going for you, it's not wise to send records randomly to stations that have no real reason to listen to it or play it. In this case, your best bet is to send records only to stations in your region or state that play your style of music. You need to get samples of the trade publications so that you can research which stations play music that is similar to yours. If you start out region-ally, it'll be a little easier for you to effectively promote your release to those stations; for instance, the phone calls will cost less. If you're planning to tour, send copies to stations along your tour route.

If you are going to take out national ads promoting your record, you can send records to hundreds of stations. With fol-low-up phone calls to the Music Directors and ads in the trades you'll be able to get stations to play your record.

The majority of college and public radio stations have specialty shows for nearly every style of music, as opposed to commercial stations which are usually one style. You're going to have much more success getting stations to play your record if you concentrate on the college and public stations. If you can get airplay on these stations, you have a better chance of the com-mercial stations adding your release to their playlist.

What To Include In Your Mail-out

Your package should consist of either one or two copies of your release, a letter to the Music Director (get his or her name out of the trade publications or simply write: Dear Music Direc-tor) introducing your group (keep it simple) and *stressing a par-ticular song.* Include a one-sheet biography containing band information and a list of the tracks on your record, and, if you'd like, a small poster, promo picture or sticker (these three are optional). Don't send copies of every time your band's name has ever appeared in print. I also don't recommend the "We've opened for Nirvana, Barry Manilow, Joe Blow, etc." approach. Who cares who you've played with. Stick to the core information about your music and, if you have any press reviews, pull some quotes out and include them in your one-sheet.

It's very important, if you are sending anything other than a single, to tell the MD which song to play. They simply don't have the time to listen to every song on your record and decide which one is the best. *Tell them.* This should be in bold, attention getting type.

Bounce-back Cards

These are stamped postcards, addressed back to you, that you include in your mail out. A typical one would ask for the station name, address, phone number and person sending it, whether or not they added your record to their playlist and what trades they report to. At 19¢ per card, it's a lot less expensive than subscribing to the trade publications. The card should read: "If you'd like to receive the upcoming new releases from _____ Records, send us this card!" Bounce back cards are the best method for finding out what stations are playing your music. When you get them back, you'll have the name of someone who actually touched your record at that station. Call them up and ask if they're playing it, what clubs your group can play in their town, if the station puts on shows, etc.

The Package

The best way to send records through the mail is in a cardboard mailer, specially made for whatever format you're sending. Whoever manufactures your album, cassette or CD can sell you these. If you're using envelopes, for God's sake man, stick a piece of cardboard in there! It's pretty pathetic to spend all this time and money, just to have your record broken en route to the station. This goes for cassettes and CDs, too.

Try to use some creativity in packaging your mail-out; colored envelopes, rubber-stamped propaganda, whatever it takes to stand out from the rest of the pack. Remember these stations get dozens of packages a day. The package should be addressed either ATTN: MUSIC DIRECTOR or the MD's name. Also, your style of music should be written clearly on the outside of your package. This makes it easier for station personnel to direct it to the appropriate DJ(s).

Timing (College Radio)

College radio stations are staffed by college students who are usually gone during summer and winter vacations. The staff is greatly reduced, and some stations close down altogether. It's *important* to send material to college radio in either the Spring or Fall.

Postage

Always use the "Special Fourth Class Sound Recording" rate. It'll take between two and ten days to get to it's destination, but it's the most cost effective way to send out your records. It will usually cost between $1 and $1.50 per record, depending how much additional material you include.

For more information on what radio station Music Directors look for in a submission, read the **Interviews** section of this book.

Trade Publications

Following this section is a list of radio trade publications in the United States. The function of these magazines is to gather the playlists from hundreds of stations and compile them into national charts. There are individual charts for all styles of music in each publication. Some list retail sales, also. These publications also feature reviews of new releases and are a forum for record label advertisements hyping those new releases.

Get Samples!

Call or write each one of these trades publications. Tell them that you're from _____ Records and that you'd like to advertise your new release in their magazine (the key word there is **advertise**). Ask for a rate card and a sample copy of their most recent issue. These trades are a valuable resource for the following reasons: One, you can easily browse through the playlists of hundreds of radio stations in order to find stations that play your style of music. Two, you'll get a feel for the kind of radio specific advertising that other independent labels are putting out. And three, most of the playlists listed in these publications include the name of the Music Director and the phone number of each station. These magazines *do not* list the station addresses; you'll have to cross reference these with the radio directory in this book. When you call these magazines, find out who to send review copies to and what their reviewing policy is in general.

What's A Tipsheet?

Trade publications are sometimes called *tipsheets.* The difference between a tipsheet and your average music review magazine is that you will never see a bad word written about a new record in a tipsheet. There are no records featured that the tipsheet does not like; it's full of good reviews. A review in one of the major trades can dramatically increase the chances of your release getting substantial airplay. Therefore, you should concentrate your efforts on getting these publications to mention your record. How do you get a review in a trade. I don't think anyone is going to come out and say it, but the reality of it is: Buy an ad = get a review. These publications are businesses. They want to reserve review space for the companies that spend big money advertising with them.

Who reads the trades? At radio stations, they're read by the Music Director, Program Director and the various DJs. Major and independent labels also read them, to see where their music is receiving airplay. This makes the trades an ideal place to advertise your release. A small ad will likely cost a few hundred dollars, but it's probably worth it if you're serious about getting your music played.

Getting Reviewed

Your first step should always be to try to get reviewed in the trades because it won't cost you anything, other than a few sample copies of your record and several phone calls. When you call to get a sample copy of a trade, find out who does the reviews. Send a copy to that person, but also send a copy to the editor, the publisher, maybe the art director, mailroom staff, who knows. If several people at the magazine are listening to your release, it increases the chance of someone actually reviewing it. Don't go overboard with this, but definitely send a few copies to each trade. And, as I mentioned before, the trades sometimes look a little more kindly upon you if you take out an ad.

Radio Specific Ads

Ads in the trades are different than ordinary music magazine ads, because they are usually directed at one person; the MD, the PD, a DJ, etc. In these ads, you'll notice lines like, "The new single, on you desk now!" and lists of the stations that are currently playing a particular track. When you get your sample copies of the trades, check out the advertisements for ideas for your ads.

Ad Timing

If you're planning to take out an advertisement in a radio trade, timing is critical. These publications come out on a weekly or bi-weekly basis. Ads in them must come out the same week that your record reaches the radio station! If not the same week, then it should at least be published the week *before* it gets there. And, if you can afford it, keep running the ad for a few weeks after.

Trade Publications

Album Network
120 N. Victory Blvd. 3rd Floor
Burbank, CA 91502
818-955-4000
(Retail and radio charts for rock and alternative rock. Published weekly, 300 reporters. Also publishes "Yellow Pages of Rock" dirtectory, yearly.)

Billboard
1515 Broadway
New York, NY 10036
1-800-669-1002
(Radio and retail, over 1000 reporters. All musical styles, including classical. Published weekly.)

CMJ New Music Report
245 Great Neck Road
Third Floor
Great Neck, NY 11021
516-466-6000
fax - 516-466-7159
(Majority of stations listed are college radio. Over 1,000 stations and retailers report weekly. Rock, rap, reggae / world music, metal, jazz, alternative. CMJ puts on yearly CMJ Music Marathon in NYC that features showcases of emerging bands. Call for details.)

The Gavin Report
140 Second Street
San Francisco, CA 94105
415-495-1990
fax - 415-495-2580
(Over 1300 reporters. Top 40, alternative, rap, contemporary,
jazz, country. Mostly commercial radio. Call for free sample.)

The Hard Report
4 Trading Post Way
Medford Lakes, NJ 08055
609-654-7272
(Radio charts for AOR, alternative, metal. Over 250 reporters,
interviews, music news, new releases. Published weekly.)

Hits
14958 Ventura Blvd.
Sherman Oaks, CA 91403
818-501-7900
(Radio and retail charts, over 700 radio stations report. Published
weekly)

Radio And Records (R&R)
1930 Century Park West
Los Angeles, CA 90067
213-553-4330
(Charts by format: Contemporary Hit Radio, Adult Contemporary,
Urban Contemporary, Jazz, New Age, Album Oriented Rock,
Country, New Rock. 1000 reporters, published weekly)

Rockpool

83 Leonard St. 2nd Floor
New York, NY 10013
212-219-0777
Fax - 212-219-0777
(Alternative rock, dance, rap, metal, reggae. College radio and independent retail. Also has radio and dance record pools. Call for info.)

Independent Promoters

If you don't want to deal with the hassle of radio promotion, here's a few independent promoters that will - for a price.

A&R Consultants	313-761-2600
AIM Marketing	201-679-9111
Beat Vision	503-234-2300
Boomerang Productions	212-941-0147
Blue Viking	818-888-3436
One Way	213-874-7222
Second Vision	212-334-9260
Set To Run	212-687-0522
Singermanagement Inc.	212-757-1217
Sky Promotions	800-442-3142
SRO	800-937-7687
Thirsty Ear	212-889-9595
The Want Ads	213-851-7519

Performance Rights Organizations

Performance rights organizations monitor radio and television broadcasts and collect royalties, which you'll recieve a share of if you are a member and your music gets played. They also collect money from businesses, such as restaurants, that play music or the radio for their customers. (There is a lot of contraversy surrounding this practice. Get the facts and decide for yourself.) The two major companies are ASCAP and BMI, and a letter to either of them will get you complete information on their services and how to join.

ASCAP

One Lincoln Plaza
New York, NY 10023

BMI

320 West 57th St.
New York, NY 10019

Interviews

Every person involved in the music industry has his or her own opinions and thoughts concerning the value of radio airplay for an emerging artist, and how to get that artist's music played. The following pages are the result of talking to: radio station Music Directors about what they want to receive and what influences their decisions on what to play; record label staff who are trying to get their music played on radio; and independent musicians who've gotten airplay and how it's helped them. Some are optimistic about the chances of unknown bands getting played. Others have doubts about the value of getting radio airplay, and the radio industry in general. Hopefully, their advice will help you to avoid the pitfalls and give you a few new ideas.

Greg Jacobs

Greg Jacobs has done radio promotion for Capitol Records, Enigma Records, SST Records and Cruz Records. He is currently Sales Manager (and still does promotion) at Cargo Records in San Diego, CA.

Interviewed by Gary Hustwit.

G.H.- What was a typical radio send-out when you were at SST or Cruz?
G.J.- Well, for Big Drill Car's *Album Type Thing* we sent out about 400 pieces total, that's for college, commercial and press. 400 to 450; 75 to press and the rest to radio. That album made Top 50 CMJ.
G.H.- How many stations did you have to actually call?
G.J.- *Every* station that got a record got a call.
G.H.- Really?
G.J.- Yeah. I called everyone I sent it to. "Did you get it? Is it warped?" You know, make sure that they got it and that it made it in good condition. Then you've got to get them to listen to it.
G.H.- What do you say?
G.J.- "Well, did you listen to it yet?" Sometimes they'll say "yes" even though they haven't. If you ask them about the record, you can tell if they've listened to it or not.
G.H.- Do you ever put self-addressed, stamped postcards,

bounce-back cards in your send-outs?

G.J.- That's what we do now at Cargo.

G.H.- Do you get them back from the stations?

G.J.- We get probably 40% to 60% back. I think the cards are good for bands that don't have a label behind them, or who can't afford the phone bills, but you're not going to get the response that you will if you call every station. You need to call every single person (Music Directors) you mailed the record to, make sure they got it and talk to them about it.

G.H.- How do you get them to report your record in the trades?

G.J.- Well, you kind of say, "So how's that doing for you? Is it in heavy rotation? Is it going to be reported?" You've got to try. It's hard to get people to move it up on the charts, but if you keep calling them, and can build a good rapport with them, sometimes they'll be willing to help you out.

G.H.- What do you think about the importance of college radio airplay to independent artists?

G.J.- I think it's vital. For an independent band, I think college radio and touring are the only ways you're going to sell records. If you can get it to the radio station, get it on the air, and get the band to play in that town; people that listen to the college radio are the people that are going to go to the show and they're the people that are going to buy the records. If you're an indie band on the road and you don't have radio support, it's going to be really hard to get people to go to your shows.

G.H.- It'd probably be hard just to get the show if you don't have a station playing the record in that town.

G.J.- Yeah. Every now and then people go off a review they read or something, but I think college radio is very important.

G.H.- What do you see as the difference between college and commercial stations when it comes to getting something played?

G.J.- Commercial is *really* hard. It's hard to even get through to the Music Director if you call.

G.H.- Do you only talk to the MD or do you talk to DJs, too.

G.J.- Most of the time you talk to the MD, but some college stations will have an Alternative MD, a Jazz MD, etc. You'll find that out by calling. I always ask for playlists when I talk to a station for the first time. If you're an indie band, you need to get the playlists, unless you can afford a subscription to CMJ.

G.H.- Or if you call CMJ every week with a different label name and ask for a sample copy and a rate card.

G.J.- Yeah, but if you can't afford CMJ ($250 a year) you should at *least* get a hold of one copy, because that gives you the station phone numbers, the MDs name and their playlist. Or if you call them you can get the full playlist with the specialty shows, light and medium rotations, etc. It's important to know what the station plays before you send your record.

G.H.- If you were starting your own label right now, and you didn't have a lot of money, would you advertise in the trades?

G.J.- I'm sure it helps, but if I was starting my own label I would definitely spend the money on phone calls to the stations. I think it's much more important to make personal contact with the MD.

G.H.- Or do both?

G.J.- Well, if you're going to do an ad in one of the trades, your timing has to be pretty good. When the MD is opening your record, he should see your ad right then, so that he'll think, "I've heard of this." Then if you can get a good review in CMJ..... college station MDs read CMJ cover to cover.

G.H.- What do you think it takes to get a review in the trades if you're an unknown artist? Is it buy an ad, get a review?

G.J.- Before you send your material, call the magazine and get a name and find out their policy for reviews so that you're not sending it in blindly. After sending it, follow up with a phone call to make sure they got it and ask them if they're going to review it.

I really don't think you can buy a review in CMJ. They're pretty good about that. Most really small indie bands won't get put with the normal reviews though, they'll get put in the F.Y.I. or the Futures sections. But people *do* read those.

G.H.- What other advice would you give a band as far as what to send to the stations?

G.J.- To radio, you can either send CD or vinyl; most college stations are CD capable now, and actually prefer it. But vinyl is still OK, people are still playing 7"s. You should also do a one-sheet promo / bio type thing as opposed to an eight page press kit, because they're more apt to look at it because it's just one sheet, not a book. Photos aren't necessary. To the press for sure, but not for radio.

G.H.- Posters?

G.J.- I've never done that. It seems more likely that they'll throw it away than put it up. I'd personally rather put that money into phone calls to the stations I sent the record to. I really think it's important to call them; more than once, if you can afford to.

G.H.- If you were starting your own label, with no previous radio contact, how many records would you send to radio? How many would you need to make an impact in the charts, but still be manageable for a new band or label?

G.J.- To chart in, say, the national top 150 of CMJ, you'd have to send at least 300 pieces.

G.H.- And get half of them to play it? A third of them?

G.J.- If you can get half of them to report it, you should have my job! (laughs)

G.H.- So you think 300 stations is manageable? That's at least $300 if you called each station just for a minute.

G.J.- It's expensive if you want to do well. If you don't want to spend all of your money on phone calls, you could put the post-cards in and only call the people that don't send them back. I call everybody, but I don't pay the phone bills. Whether they return the cards or not, it's important to call them.

G.H.- What do your postcards say on them?

G.J.- They list whatever records came in the box, and after each record it says, "Do you get it in good condition? Is it receiving light, medium or heavy rotation? Will it be reported?" Like I said before, about 40% come back. If you can get 100 stations to report your record, you'll be doing great.

Marco Collins

Marco Collins is the Music Director at KNDD, a commercial, alternative station in Seattle, Washington.

Interviewed by Gary Hustwit.

G.H.- What's your advice to bands that are trying to get played on commercial stations? Is it impossible?
M.C.- No. I think that it's becoming more and more feasible all the time.
G.H.- What about formats?
M.C.- Obviously, the best format for radio is CD, vinyl after that, and cassettes are the most difficult to deal with. It'd be better to send a quarter-inch reel than a cassette.
G.H.- What else should they send you?
M.C.- Information about the artist, so that when I listen to the music I know what the band's about. A bio, a photo, cool packaging; I think that throwing something in to spark the attention of the MD or PD is always beneficial. You don't have to spend thousands of dollars delivering pizzas to us or anything. You need something to get attention so that your record doesn't get thrown into some *other* huge stack. What bands need to realize is that MDs are inundated with so much new music; that whether or not

they want to stay true to their roots and listen to everything, there's no way possible that they're going to get the chance to listen to everything that's sent to them.

G.H.- How many submissions do you get per week?

M.C.- Probably around 200.

G.H.- Do you have someone who helps you sort through it?

M.C.- No, I listen to it all.

G.H.- You seriously listen to everything?

M.C.- Well, there are some things that I don't always have time to listen to; that's why packaging plays a big part. I would *love* to listen to everything, but when I come into my office every day and I have *crates* of records that have come in, I don't have time to go through it all. So, I go through the things that jump out at me and the things I'm familiar with or have read about. I do sit down and sort through a lot of the smaller stuff a lot more than most MDs, because of my background with Loudspeaker (a local music show). I know that you can find a lot of gems in the rough.

G.H.- Do you think bands should advertise in the trades? Would that spark your interest?

M.C.- I don't know if advertising, dropping cash, is the most important thing to do. There are ways of dealing with the trades, like getting them to send out your records for you. Rockpool and CMJ have record pools where, if they like your record, they'll send it out to stations. Those magazines are good at not letting the little guy slip by. I've seen reviews of cassette only releases on the covers of those magazines. It's important not to ignore the trades, but I don't know if dropping cash is beneficial.

G.H.- What trades do you read regularly?

M.C.- Just about everything; R&R, CMJ, Rockpool, Album Network, Hits, Gavin, Hard Report, Billboard.

G.H.- What about follow-up calls after the band has sent their records?

M.C.- Oh, yeah, that's important, too. You know, it's a horrible thing to say, but the quality of the music is a very small part of getting airplay. There are so many other things that have to be dealt with before you're going to get close to having people take your music seriously. If you're going to send out stuff to radio stations, make sure that you're going to be able to do some sort of follow up work on it. You need to be able to call stations around the country and make sure that they're playing your record, make sure that they at least got your record. If you can't afford calling, even correspondence by mail is better than nothing.

G.H.- Any other advice for bands?

M.C.- To bands that are on the indie level, struggling to get their music out there, to me the important thing to focus on is not trying to get in regular rotation at a commercial station, but to focus on the specialty shows. These shows are there to expose new music. Don't necessarily focus on the Music Director of the entire station; focus on the hosts of the specialty shows. Call the stations, find out what their format is about, when they will take risks and play new bands or cassettes. Find out who the hosts of those shows are, and send your record to them. Do your home-work, don't just send things out blindly. Find out who is respon-sible for actually getting the stuff on the air. And in addition to servicing the stations, make sure you send review copies to all the trades.

Kane

Kane runs Headhunter Records, an independent label in San Diego, CA.

Interviewed by Gary Hustwit.

G.H.- You just stated that you don't like college radio.
K.- Well, the only college radio stations I ever sent records to were certain big ones, like KXLU in L.A. Other than that I've always thought it was a waste of time.
G.H.- So you'd send to the bigger, broadcast stations?
K.- Yeah, ones that have people listening to them, not some little, shitty hardcore show at three in the morning. I used to deal directly with a lot of record stores, so I'd call up a store and ask them what were the college stations in their area, and if it was worthwhile to send to them or not. I try to talk to people who live in the area and listen to the station, people who's opinion I value or who work at a store, etc. I'd rather send a record to a store for in-store play than to some little station in Omaha, Nebraska or something.
G.H.- Has college radio airplay helped any of the bands that you've worked with? As far as getting shows in that town, etc?
K.- There's a few good stations; one in Berkeley, and in L.A. it

helps. Rarely have I gotten a letter from someone buying a record saying that they heard it on college radio. Our radio mailing list, If I had my way, would be about 40 stations. To me, the CMJ charts mean nothing, unless you can get it up really high, and that takes a lot of time and money. If it's not in the top 20 it's meaningless. I think there are good college radio stations but they're few and far between, and most of the playlists I've seen are full of crappy, major label stuff. It's like, what's next for these college stations; are they going to be oldies stations or something?

G.H.- So if a band is going to send out to college radio, they should try to pinpoint the better stations?

K.- You have to find the good towns, and talk to a lot of people. Don't just get a CMJ chart and blindly send out 400 copies.

G.H.- What were the numbers for a recent Headhunter mail-out?

K.- Well, for Drive Like Jehu we sent to about 200 college stations.

G.H.- Did you call them all?

K.- No, we sent postcards with the records. We call very few of them. Shadowy Men On A Shadowy Planet's last album was #43 on CMJ, a lot of stations played that.

G.H.- So for a developing band, do you think college radio has any importance at all?

K.- It's important for some cities, it's very important for L.A., Berkeley, New York and the bigger markets. But if a band doesn't have the resources, they shouldn't waste their money sending to the smaller cities, unless they have the time and money to call the stations. If you're going to do it, you have to go all out, and call, and do it right. But if it's your first record and you send it out and don't call or follow-up on it, you've just wasted your money. I'd just concentrate on the best 30 or 40 stations.

G.H.- I've heard of bands getting 20 or 30 stations to play their

record, and then they were able to set up national tours just from that airplay.

K.- Well, I've always had a bad attitude towards college stations from day one; especially these elitist college students working there. I've always gone the route of talking to people in stores, finding out what are the good stores in the neighborhood. These stores will usually post fliers for you, and the people at the stores know the scene more, and they're usually not college students. I think that the major labels have ruined it (college radio) in a way; a lot of times it goes to the college student's head that the major labels are calling them and sending them tickets to shows, etc. I think that they're a lot more selective concerning the independents they add; they're more interested in what's cool or hip rather than what's interesting sounding or different.

G.H.- They usually just play what's already in the charts?

K.- Yeah, I don't think that there are many Music Directors or DJs that will play something that they think is cool or different instead of what everybody tells them they should play. Especially the reporting; I'm sure that most of the stuff that's getting reported isn't getting played. They're just reporting it because someone (record label) *wants* them to report it. I used to work for a company in L.A. that did a lot of country music, and it was a scam. They got this guy who was a big Nashville producer, and he'd charge these little, no-name country acts $5000 to get their single charting in the Billboard country charts. He wouldn't even send the records out; the stations would report it for him and sure enough, it'd chart in Billboard. He'd fly these DJs to Vegas and send them prostitutes, and he'd do enough favors for them that they'd do him a favor and report his single. He did a couple of those a month. It's definitely to a much lesser degree at the college stations, they're not sending them prostitutes or anything.

G.H.- I *have* heard of MDs getting flown to London, or some-

where, to see this new major label band.

K.- Yeah, if someone has done a lot of favors for them, they'll just ask them to report their records.

G.H.- When you do send-outs, do you send vinyl or CDs?

K.- Mostly CDs now; most college radio still plays vinyl, but we're sending more and more CDs. On a lot of our releases we're not even doing vinyl.

G.H.- Do you take out ads in the trades?

K.- I hate running ads in the trades; to me, it's a waste of money. They're just schmooze magazines. If I'm going to advertise, I'll advertise in magazines that people buy records from. People who read Rockpool don't buy records, they just get someone to send them one.

G.H.- But if a band has zero previous exposure, do you think ads have any bearing on getting played?

K.- Well, a zero band probably doesn't have enough money to advertise in CMJ. They have to have a lot of money behind them, and be sure that the record's going to sell to make the money back. You could run a lot of ads in, say, Flipside for the same amount of money as one in CMJ. Certain bands do better in college radio; it really depends on your music, the timing and what's popular. It can help, but the majority of the time I think it's a waste of money. Start off with a small number of stations and work from that. If you can get a lot of reviews, stations will call you and ask for a copy.

Pete Kellers

Pete Kellers is the Music Director at KSDT, University of California at San Diego. He's been the MD for the past year; prior to that he was a DJ for three years at UCSD and Texas A&M.

Interviewed by Gary Hustwit.

G.H.- How many different types of music are played on KSDT?
P.K.- Just about everything. We have a metal show, a few rap shows, a reggae show, and the DJs are encouraged to play all the various kinds of music during their regular shows.
G.H.- Jazz?
P.K.- There's a couple jazz shows. Industrial, folk, everything.
G.H.- How many records do you receive at the station each week?
P.K.- 30 to 40 a week. We probably add about a third of those. We get sent mostly CDs now, records are almost a thing of the past. We're getting a *lot* more CDs, but I'm more likely to listen to vinyl more closely, because I'd rather add that than CDs, since we get so few vinyl records.
G.H.- Do you still play all your old vinyl?
P.K.- Yeah. We have about 100,000 vinyl records and we still have turntables. We only started adding CDs about a year or two ago.

G.H.- What about cassettes?

P.K.- Cassettes are a pain in the ass. They're really hard to play, really hard to cue up on the air, so they basically hardly *ever* get played. We have some, like local bands that we like to support, but we hardly play cassettes.

G.H.- Do the record label people pressure you to play their stuff?

P.K.- No, most people are pretty cool. The worst is when it's some band that you can't stand, that's really horrible. They'll call you and say, "Hey, have you listened to this or that?" and I'll say, "Well yeah, and I don't think it's really what we want to play here." Then they'll say, "Oh, come on, have you listened to this track and that track, etc. We're going for adds this week." And I'm just like, "Get off my back!" If it's a record that you really don't like, then badgering you just makes it worse. If it's a medium record, badgering helps, I guess.

G.H.- Has anyone offered to fly you to New York to see a band or anything like that?

P.K.- Well, I know that at big commercial stations, they get all kinds of crap, they get anything they want. We get lots of stuff, like I can call just about any label and ask for an extra copy of something, or tickets to shows.

G.H.- Of the promo calls that you get, how many of them are from major labels as opposed to indies?

P.K.- Some of the majors, like Sony, have a big group of promo people. A&M does a lot of radio tracking, but Warner Brothers doesn't. Most independent labels don't track either. Some labels either know that everyone's going to play it or they just don't need to find out from you, they can read the trades.

G.H.- What should an independent band or artist send you?

P.K.- Basically, if they send a tape, they're *doomed.* I can't listen to a whole tape, you know? I can sample individual songs on a record, or a CD, but I can't sit down and listen to a whole tape, it's too much. So they should send CD or vinyl; seven inches are good, twelve inches are good. They should send a little letter, not a bunch of weird shit, just a letter that says, "Hi, we're from this or that, we're putting this record out ourselves, please play it." I get a lot of stickers and things, which are pretty cool, but it's usually like, "Who the hell is this?" If the music's good, I'll add it, if it's not, I won't. I listen to everything, and I don't always look to see what label it's on before I play it. If it's just a record and I don't know where it's from, I'll play it. If it's a tape and I don't know where it's from, I probably won't play it.

G.H.- Do you read CMJ and Rockpool and the other trades?

P.K.- Yeah, I do.

G.H.- If you see an advertisement from some band you've never heard of, and then you get their record that week, are you more likely to listen to it?

P.K.- Probably. But I'd most likely play it if they (the trades) reviewed it. I also read them to make sure we're getting all the new releases from labels. Bands should definitely send their stuff to CMJ and Rockpool and the other trades.

G.H.- Do you get The Gavin Report at your station?

P.K.- No, we don't subscribe to the Gavin, because it's really expensive, and it's mostly major labels and big commercial stations. I guess bands should send something to them, but I don't think they're going to take you too seriously. The trades probably feel the same way as radio, concerning tapes vs. vinyl, etc. I've seen a lot of local bands in CMJ, so bands should definitely send to the trades. People read them.

G.H.- If bands call you and ask you to send them playlists, will you send them?

P.K.- If it's a label we will, but if it's a band, probably not. We don't have enough money to send out tons of playlists, so we have to decide who's on our mailing list and who's not.

G.H.- But if a band wanted a single playlist, just to see the type of music you play?

P.K.- If they were nice on the phone I probably would. If they were annoying I probably wouldn't bother.

G.H.- Do you think it's worth it for a band to try to get college radio airplay?

P.K.- Yeah, totally. For example, there was this band, Psychefunkapus, that sent us a CD they put out themselves. There was a letter with it that said, "Please....we spent all our money on this....play it." We listened to it and it was kind of cool. The next thing you know, they get picked up by Atlantic. If a band gets reviewed in CMJ, labels read that stuff, too. I think it's definitely worth it (to try to get airplay), but only if you're going to be serious about it.

Doug Moody

Doug Moody started Mystic Studios in 1968 in Hollywood, and has recorded and promoted hundreds of bands of all styles. In 1986 he started Mystic Records.

Interviewed by Gary Hustwit.

G.H.- Is it worth it for bands who are just starting out to send their records to radio stations and take out ads in the trades?
D.M.- First of all I'm not in a band, I have a label. So I have to speak from the standpoint of a label. The majority of bands that are putting out records, they don't mind if they lose their shirts because what they're after is publicity for the band name. There's a difference between a record label which is trying to build the label and a continuing line of product and a band that's putting out a product. So for a band, *any* money that it spends to get its name on the air or in a review is worthwhile, because it's promoting a band. For a label, it's not worthwhile because it's not selective enough. My attitude towards college radio is unless you're in touch with a person (at the radio station) who understands your label concept and has a passion for the type of music you're putting out, then college radio is usually a waste of time. College radio stations are usually staffed by young people who are influenced by the major (label) corporations, and they're looking for

jobs at those major corporations.

G.H.- So you think that if someone at a college station is trying to get a job with say, Geffen, that they're going to play or program mostly Geffen's product?

D.M.- Well, everyone's going to kiss ass, and put out bits of paper (playlists). I've known instances where you get on a mailing list from a college station, and since we have several different mailing addresses we've gotten *different* Top 40 lists from the same station! They just run them off on their xerox machines and sent them out to please you so that they get more of your records and get on your label's mailing list. What's a piece of xeroxed paper? It tells you what you want to see. It's just like print media, you pay for an ad that pleases you, and the publicity may rub off somewhere else. To go on again about that college radio question, for the past six years I've promoted what is called thrash music, an offshoot of hardcore punk and speedmetal, more of a white ghetto music as opposed to rap. Some of the college stations have exposed Mystic records over the past five years; bands like Government Issue, NOFX, R.K.L., Ill Repute. But most of the stations have never played any thrash music until recently, when, out of Seattle, bands like Nirvana go platinum doing thrash music. College radio is jumping on the bandwagon without understanding what the roots are about because they never played thrash music in the first place. They're playing something that is now publicly acceptable. College radio, to my mind, has *never* exposed new music. I know that's a broad statement, but that's my opinion.

G.H.- Only when major labels put out something do the college stations play it?

D.M.- College radio is a tool of the major labels today, more than it is for independents, and of course that's the fault of distribution. The large distributors don't seem to carry much independent product anymore, they carry only that which is supported and advertised by majors, and the major corporations *do* control most of the display space in the chains. If you've got control and access to 30,000 Wherehouse stores or Sam Goody or whatever, you don't want little shitty independents in the store! Unless a major record company has a hand in these small labels or is financing these small labels, very rarely do you find small labels in chain stores today.

G.H.- The major labels are going to try to squeeze the independents out of radio and retail?

D.M.- Always have. The difference between an independent label and a band is that the label is trying to *stay* independent, whereas the band putting out a single record is trying to jump on to a major.

G.H.- Or maybe start it's own independent label?

D.M.- Well, yeah it could start it's own independent label but I'm sure it wouldn't want to sustain it. If the band ended up getting a world tour, it wouldn't have time to run it's own record company. Hardly any major group has ever run it's own label, it's done a deal through a major. *You* were associated with an independent label, SST, that has tried to stay independent. What happens is that the groups leave, and go to majors.

G.H.- If you had to give advice to a band that's trying to get exposure for its music, what would it be?

D.M.- First of all, go to your local public access TV stations. In the next few years, visual records are *definitely* coming in. The Phillips Corporation, in Europe, has put out cassette tapes that you can play on your TV, and Sony has the mini-disc that plays on TV, whatever the format is, you're going to be dealing with visual records. You have to learn to present yourself *visually*. The second thing is you've got to start touring. If you're a band that lives at home or has some sort of support; unlike years ago groups like the Police would stay on the road forever, or Fugazi; they live like monks and they stay *out there*, you know? Whether there's 200 people that'll pay to see them or 50 people; they'll play every night. Those kind of groups are rare these days. Those are the groups that will be out there for ten years. Any other group usually has a job, and they only want to play weekends until they're sure that they've got an income from music. The obvious thing they should go for is exposure, and public access TV is you're best bet right now because they *have* to give you access, they *have* to expose you. It's amazing how many people actually watch those local public access stations.

As for radio, by all means if you've got the money go into Rockpool, go into CMJ, go into anything you can. And also, watch *European* radio; you've got 100 million people over there who'll buy anything that comes from America. In England, and especially Germany, the chance for a group to grow is better than in America.

Phyllis Hegeman

Phyllis Hegeman is the Music Director at KSDS Jazz 88FM in San Diego.

Interviewed by Gary Hustwit.

G.H.- Will your station play music from a completely unknown artist?
P.H.- Well, in the interest of broadcast sound quality, we can't air material unless it's on LP or CD, but I do listen to every track from every release I receive, I don't skip anything just because I don't know it or I don't know the label, but I could be an exception (among MDs). I guess I start with the recording quality; obviously it has to be great. Given that the recording quality and musician-ship are there and everything sounds good, we really just go off of the sound and whether or not it fits our format. We happen to have a full-spectrum jazz format, in that all forms of jazz are airable on our station. There are so many different kinds of jazz; big band, classic, vintage, modern contemporary jazz, fusion and everything in between. We also have latin and world beat shows.
G.H.- How many submissions do you get a week?
P.H.- It varies from about 10 to 80 a week.
G.H.- Are the majority of the releases you receive on vinyl or

CD?

P.H.- It's almost all CD. No one ever sends vinyl anymore, it's maybe one in a thousand.

G.H.- Do you still play your old vinyl?

P.H.- We sure do. Actually, I'm in the process of going through 8000 LPs that we have and washing them and listening to them to make sure we still want to air them.

G.H.- So a vinyl release would almost stand out if it was sent to you?

P.H.- Sure! "Look, it's a record!" People just don't do it anymore. Our station can air them, but I imagine there are some stations that don't even use their turntables.

G.H.- A lot of the alternative rock / college radio type labels still put out vinyl.

P.H.- Well, jazz is also different because the songs don't have to go by a formula; I prefer the longer selections, seven and eight minute tunes not three and a half minutes like rock songs always use. The longer songs give the musician a chance to really stretch out and show their stuff which is what jazz is about; improvisation. It's also easier for the DJ to play five to eight minute tunes instead of a bunch of three minute tunes. I think *live* albums are great, if there's anything I have to say it'd be that if you can get a good quality sound, I think live has something to say that the rest (studio recorded) can't. For me, live is where it's at. I mean, there are a lot of wonderful recordings that aren't live, but the energy is often different.

G.H.- Does your station report to the trades?

P.H.- Yes we do. We report to Radio & Records, Gavin, MAC Report and Jazziz Magazine.

G.H.- Do you read them personally?

P.H.- Yeah, we receive R & R and the Gavin, and we have to stay up what's happening. We do a show called Friday Night Countdown, where we play the top songs according to our thoughts, our DJs' airplay and also how they're doing on the charts.

G.H.- What if you saw a review of a group that you've never heard of?

P.H.- If it was a *great* review, I'd look into it. We go on some of what the media puts out, but to me that's only a suggestion. I go by my own ears. So does Tony (Sisti, the Program Director), and we're both musicians; it's not like we're just anybody sitting here making judgements about music.

G.H.- Besides the recording, what should independent artists include in their mailing to your station?

P.H.- A biography and a review would be good.

G.H.- What about follow-up phone calls?

P.H.- It's a good idea if they can afford to do it; to make sure we received it, to make sure we listen to it. One little nudge is always good, because if we haven't received it or we haven't listened to it yet, it forces us to get it out right then and listen to it. As far as the music goes, it has to be creative, or a little different, but still within the jazz realm.

G.H.- So it doesn't matter what label it's on?

P.H.- No. A lot of times the independents have more room to be creative. My advice to musicians trying to get on radio is to go to the radio conventions, and jazz artists should go to the International Association of Jazz Educators Convention. They have to be creative and have a unique, *distinct* sound on their instrument. Those are pretty much the *most* important things.

Amy Davis

Amy Davis was the Music Director from '88 to '91 at WMWM, Salem State University in Salem, Massachusetts.

Interviewed by Gary Hustwit.

G.H.- You were the MD at WMWM for three years. What musical styles did you play there?
A.D.- Alternative rock and, during the last year, rock and rap.
G.H.- Did you play more vinyl or more CDs?
A.D.- Mostly vinyl, but in the last two years we were playing more CDs. People weren't as apt to play the CDs at first; I think that's less of a problem now. People were almost afraid of them at first.
G.H.- A lot of the independent labels still put out vinyl...
A.D.- Which is wonderful. I think it's great, because there are people who still want it. I just like to *play* the vinyl better. Never cassettes, they're the worst. Unless you've got someone who wants to sit there and listen to all these cassettes and put them onto a cart, it's a complete hassle.
G.H.- How many submissions did you receive a week?
A.D.- 50 to 100 a week. Everything from the major labels to the tiniest band putting out their own thing. The independents would

send vinyl, but the majors were all CDs.

G.H.- When you looked at the stack of records that had been mailed to you each week, how did you decide what to listen to?

A.D.- Well, I'd try to skip through everything, but the titles and covers are what I look to first. But I would give everything a chance.

G.H.- For bands that are putting out their own record, what do you suggest they include in their send-out?

A.D.- Vinyl or CD and a *short* biography; not one of these twenty-five page, oh my God you're wasting a whole tree for this silly thing. No one's going to read the whole thing. There's so much stuff coming in there every day that it's impossible to read everything. They should call; about a week or week and a half after we receive it, because there was always a backlog. Ideally, if that was my only job and that's all I was doing all day, I would check out things the second they arrived. But in college radio, you're in college. So they should call, about a week or two later. It makes me aware of it; without a call their record might slip by.

G.H.- What about the trades?

A.D.- I think it's a good idea to take out an ad, even if it's a small ad. The ad puts it in the MD's mind, even if it comes out a week or two before the record gets to the station. It's strikes a chord in you memory. I feel that I'd be more likely to check it out.

G.H.- Tell me about some of the promo people you've encountered.

A.D.- Some of them were bad, they'd just call and call and call and call. They can be completely pushy. Some people would say, "If you don't do this for me, I'll never talk to you again." It all depends on the person, but some major labels get completely out of hand. I think some organizations did a really great job, like AAM (an independent promoter) out of New York. If you can afford an independent promoter, I think that it has it's advantages, especially if it's a promoter that already has relationships set up with the stations.

G.H.- Any last word of advice for musicians trying to get played on radio?

A.D.- Don't be obnoxious when you call; be persistent, but in a nice way. Don't call every week; call maybe every couple of weeks. Don't get discouraged. If you believe in what you're doing, just keep going.

Noelle Giuffrida

Noelle Giuffrida is in charge of radio promotion at Touch and Go, an independent label in Chicago, IL.

Interviewed by Gary Hustwit.

G.H.- Do you think that college and public radio is important for an unknown band? Is it worth it for a band to spend the money to send out to radio?
N.G.- I think sending to a limited number of stations makes a lot of sense. To send to everyone who reports to CMJ, or to send more than 200 or 250 records, is wasteful. Keep your send-outs small. If a band is starting a label with some friends of theirs, putting out a seven inch here and there, or if a band is just releasing their own record, I'd say mail it to 50 or 60 stations. Even if you have the money, don't mail out to more than 200 or so. There's about 100 stations that are really going to pay attention to independent releases and support them if they like them. There's another 100 that are sort of hit or miss, and the rest are pretty worthless.
G.H.- What about trade publications?
N.G.- I think sending to the trades is helpful; if you send to Billboard and R&R you probably won't get much response, though.

But, then again, if you send them a cassette they might listen to it and they might like it. I think it's worth sending a cassette, but I don't think you should send multiple CD copies to everyone. CMJ, Rockpool and The Hard Report are all excellent publications that do give space to everything that is musically viable.

G.H.- What's a typical radio send-out at Touch and Go?

N.G.- To college radio, we send 275 copies; 100 of which are CDs, the rest are vinyl. We also service about 30 commercial stations.

G.H.- Do you follow up with phone calls?

N.G.- We include reply cards with postage on them. People can say what they think of the records; there's a comment space. Are you going to play this record? Yes or no. What'd you think of it on a scale of 1 to 5? Is it in heavy, medium or light rotation? It's basically for people who don't have office hours or don't have time to talk to independent labels. We also send things to Newfoundland and places where we would never call, so the response cards work, and they also show you who cares enough to bother. If they never send response cards back that have the postage on them already, if they can't take the time to do that, then they're probably not interested in independent music. At a label like ours, I don't call college radio stations once a week and say, "How's it doing this week? What rotation is it in? Can you move it up? Can I send you 10 cassettes? Can I send you 10 CDs? Do you want a free T-shirt?" That's not what it's about. I call, and my interns call, college radio once before a new release comes out, and once after it's sent to make sure it got there. I encourage them (MDs) to listen to it, and usually call them again, a couple weeks later, to see how the DJs liked it. If they're really excited about it, I'll see if the school books shows, or when the band is touring if they'd want to do an interview. It's up to them, we don't force people to do that.

G.H.- Do you think college radio airplay sells records?

N.G.- No, I don't think it sells records. There's a couple of stations that influence whether or not a band gets booked into a certain town, and I think that touring sells records. But the band may not have gotten a chance to play in that town without college radio's support. If you want to play in Columbia, MO or you want to play Chicago, and you don't have radio play on KCOU or WNUR it's more difficult. There's probably 30 or 40 stations that qualify as important for their "market." Other than that, a lot of the people who work in college radio also work in record stores. I don't think that being #1 at a certain college station sells X amount of records.

G.H.- Any other advice for bands sending their records to radio?

N.G.- Give people as much information as possible; tell them about the band, but don't make it to hypey. Look at peoples' playlists before you send your records; if they're playing Nirvana or Guns 'N Roses or a lot of major label stuff, chances are they're not going to be interested in your record. They're not going to have time, unless you're calling them every week, and they're not going to give it any significant airplay. Don't send it to commercial stations unless you're a personal friend of the DJ, because no one will ever listen to it; they'll sell it or throw it out. Be informed and use your money wisely.

The Charms

The Charms are a Southern California-based rock band that has released two independent records and gotten them played on college, public and commercial stations. They've also booked two nationwide tours with the help of college radio.

Interview with Bill Jennings of The Charms by Gary Hustwit.

G.H.- You've been played on college and public radio and you've toured due to it. What do you think of the importance of college and public radio airplay?
B.J.- I think that it's the *most* important tool an independent band has for getting shows and selling records. For a band of our stature to get on commercial radio is virtually impossible, unless it's on some special local show. College radio couldn't be more important; for playing the music, on-air interviews, presenting shows.
G.H.- So you've found that people at the stations are pretty receptive?
B.J.- I can't really think of any bad experiences. I've definitely seen a change since the first time we toured ('89), it seems like it's kind of grown up since then. People (labels) are paying so much more attention to it now. When we first went out, the stations were a little more loose, there wasn't such a rigid format to what was getting played.

G.H.- How many copies of your first record did you send to radio?

B.J.- Rockpool distributed about 80, and we sent about 150 ourselves. We were able to get about 35 stations to play it in heavy or medium rotation, and we got a few number ones.

G.H.- Did you call the stations you sent to?

B.J.- No, we just watched the trades, and when we saw someone reporting it, we'd call them and ask what were the good clubs in their town or if they'd present a show. You can find out a lot through college radio about what's going on in that town. The people at the stations are definitely the most interested in new music. Once you talk to the MDs and PDs and DJs at a station, they're usually linked to the record store owners, the club owners and the kind of crowd you want to draw in that town. For our second record, we sent out more copies, but our tracking system wasn't as good. We also made the mistake of sending out during the summer, and there just isn't anybody there. We still received enough airplay to do a second tour, though.

G.H.- What formats did you send?

B.J.- The first time we sent vinyl; the second time we sent CDs. Vinyl seemed to help because it was bigger, it was harder to steal and easier to see.

G.H.- What else do you include in your send-outs?

B.J.- Posters, bios, photos; it depends. Any kind of promo material bands can send out helps. If you have something that they can hang up at the station or stick on their car, it helps keep your band on their mind.

G.H.- What about ads in the trades?

B.J.- For the first record we had quarter-pages in Rockpool and CMJ, and I think it helped, because they (MDs) saw the name, and when our package got there they remembered it. Bands should also think about advertising in the smaller local or regional music magazines.

G.H.- When they're touring?

B.J.- No, before they go out. If you can put out ads while you're trying to get airplay and get shows, you'll have a little more support when you get out there.

G.H.- Can college radio airplay sell records?

B.J.- Yes, but just sending a record to a station won't do it. You have to get a list of the local ma & pa record stores and contact them and try to arrange to have a few copies for sale in those stores. If people hear it on radio, they may buy it or go to your show.

G.H.- Have you gotten letters from people who've heard your record on the radio and wanted to buy it?

B.J.- Yeah, definitely. A few, not a whole lot, and a lot of times it was people who were friends of people who worked at the station.

G.H.- Has airplay helped you get gigs?

B.J.- If you get played it can help you book a tour, because you can say that you're being played on a station. You can tell the club owner that you're getting extensive play, and that you'll draw people to the show. If they want, they can talk to the station to prove it. It gives you a little more clout with the club owner if your record's in rotation.

G.H.- For your next record, what format will you send to radio?

B.J.- If it's a full length record, we'll probably send a CD. If it's and EP or single, 12" vinyl.

G.H.- What did you sell when you were touring?

B.J.- We had CDs and tapes, and we definitely sold more CDs. That paid for a lot of gas, if you sell three CDs that's $30 worth of gas. It helps a lot. Another thing, if a band is set up to do it, is to play live over the air or do an interview. If a station plays your song, that's great; but if you're *in* the station, on the air, you can have 20 minutes of airtime. Just getting your music played is great, though. Hearing your song over the air is quite a payoff for the hours or years you've spent working on your music.

Radio Station Directory

      The following is a list of 900 radio stations in the U.S. and Canada. The majority of the stations are college radio and are identified by the college name in their address. The rest are either public or commercial. I cannot stress enough the importance of getting sample copies of the trade magazines before you send your records to radio stations. The trades give each station's playlist. Find out which stations play your type of music and look up their addresses in this directory. Only send to as many stations as you can call and keep in close contact with.

CANADA

CKLN-FM
380 Victoria St.
Toronto, Ontario
Canada M5b 1w7

CRSG
1455 DeMaisonneuve #647
Montreal, Quebec
Canada H3G 1M8

CITR
6138 SUB Blvd.
Vancouver, B.C.
Canada V6T 2A5

CKIC / Radio Acadia - md
Box 1269
Wolfville, NS
Canada BOP 1X0

CFUV
University of Victoria
PO Box 1700
Victoria B.C.
Canada V8W 2Y2

CFLR
Laurentian University
Sudbury, Ontario
Canada P3E 2C6

CFRC Radio,
Carruther's Hall
Queens University
Kingston, Ont.
Canada K7L 3N6

CHEZ-FM
126 York St.
Ottawa, Ont.
Canada K1N 5T5

CFOU-md
85 University Ste. 227
Ottawa, Ontario
Canada K1N 6N5

CFRU-FM
Univ. of Guelph Level 2 U.C.
Guelph, Ont.
Canada N1G 2W1

CKMS-FM
200 University Ave. W
Waterloo, Ontario
Canada N2l 3G1

ALABAMA

WUAL
University of Alabama
Tuscaloosa   AL   35486

WVUA
University of Alabama
P.O. Box 870152
Tuscaloosa   AL   35487

WLRH-FM
4701 Univ. Dr.
UAH Campus
Huntsville   AL   35899

WTOH
4000 Dauphin St.
Mobile   AL   36608

WEGL-md
1239 Haley Ctr.
Auburn University
Auburn   AL   36849

ALASKA

KRKN-md
3700 Wonderland Dr #300
Anchorage   AK   99517

KSKA FM 91-md
4101 University Dr.
Anchorage   AK   99508

KMPS-md
3211 Providence Dr.
CAS125
University of Alaska
Anchorage   AK   99508

KPXR-md
3700 Woodland #300
Anchorage   AK   99517

KBBI-md
215 E. Main Ct.
Homer, AK   99603

KSUA-md
Box 83831
Fairbanks   AK   99701

KTOO-md
224 Fourth St.
Juneau   AK   99801

KCAW-md
102 Lincoln St.
Sitka   AK   99835

KBRD FM-md
716 Totem Way
Ketchikan   AK   99901

ARIZONA

KEYX -md
218 West Hampton Ave.
Mesa   AZ 85202

KUPD-md
1900 W. Carmen
Tempe AZ 85283

KUKQ-md
1900 W. Carmen
Tempe AZ 85283

KASR-md
Arizona State University
Tempe AZ 85287

KXCI -md
220 S. 4th Ave.
Tuscon AZ 85701

KAMP-md
S.U.P.O Box 10,000
University of Arizona
Tuscon AZ 85720

KFLI-md
32000 N. Willow Creek Rd.
Embry Riddle Aeronautical
University
Prescott AZ 86301

ARKANSAS

KHDX-md
Hendrix College
Conway   AR 72032

KABF-md
1501 Arch St.
Little Rock AR 72202

KMJX-md
11101 Anderson Dr.
Little Rock AR 72212

KRFA-md
University of Arkansas
103 N. Duncan
Fayetteville AR 72701

CALIFORNIA

KLA -md
UCLA
308 Westwood Plaza
L.A. CA 90024

KXLU -md
Loyola Marymount Univ.
7101 W 80th St.
L.A. CA 90045

NPR/L.A. Bureau
12233 Olympic Bl. #130
L.A.   CA 90064

KSCR -md
USC
404 Student Union
L.A.   CA 90084

KMBU-md
Pepperdine University
Malibu   CA 90265

KCRW -md
1900 Pico Blvd
Santa Monica   CA 90405

KWTR-md
Whittier College
P.O. Box 634
Whittier   CA 90608

KBBK-md
Biola University
13800 Biola Ave.
La Mirada   CA 90639

KCEB-md
Cerritos College
11110 E. Alondra Bl.
Norwalk   CA 90650

KNAC-md
100 Oceangate P-70
Long Beach   CA 90802

KLBC-md
Long Beach College
4901 E. Carson
Long Beach   CA 90808

KLON FM
1288 Bellflower Bl.
Long Beach   CA 90815

KPCC -md
Pasadena City Coll.
1570 E Colorado Blvd.
Pasadena   CA 91106

KCSN-md
Cal. State Northridge
18111 Nordhoff St.
Northridge   CA 91330

KCLU-md
California Lutheran College
60 W. Olsen Rd.
Thousand Oaks   CA 91360

KROQ -md
3500 W. Olive Ave.
Suite 900
Burbank   CA 91505

KSPC-md
Pomona College
340 N. College
Thatcher Bldg.
Claremont   CA   91711

KSPC-md
Pamona College
340 N. College Ave
Claremont   CA   91711

KULV-md
University of LaVerne
1950 Third St.
LaVerne   CA   91750

KSAK-md
1100 N Grand Ave.
Walnut   CA   91789

KGCR-md
Grossmont College
8800 Grossmont College Dr.
El Cajon   CA   92020

KKSM-md
Palomar Coll.
1140 W. Mission Rd.
San Marcos   CA   92069

KSDT-md
UCSD-B015
La Jolla   CA   92093

91X-FM -md
4891 Pacific Coast Hwy
San Diego   CA   92110

KPBS-md
San Diego State University
San Diego   CA   92182

KCR-md
SDSU
San Diego   CA   92182

KCHV-md
Drawer II
Indio   CA   92202

KUOR-md
1200 E Coltan Ave
Redlands   CA   92374

KSSB-FM-md
CSUSB
5500 Univ. Pkwy.
San Bernadino   CA   92407

KUCR-md
UC Riverside
Riverside   CA   92521

KFCR-md
Fullerton City Coll.
321 E Chapman Ave.
Fullerton   CA   92634

KNAB-md
Chapman College
333 N. Glassel St.
Orange   CA   92666

KSBR-md
Saddleback Coll.,Box 3420
Mission Viejo   CA   92690

KUCI-md
UC Irvine
Box 4362
Irvine   CA   92716

KCSB-md
UCSB
Box 13401
Santa Barbara   CA   93107

KJUC-md
UCSB
UCEN Room 3185A
Santa Barbara   CA   93107

KTYD-md
5360 Hollister Ave.
Santa Barbara   CA   92716

KBCC-FM-md
1801 Panorama Dr.
Bakersfield   CA   93305

KCBX-md
4100 Vachell Ln.
San Luis Obispo   CA   93401

KGUR-md
Cuesta College
P.O. Box 8106
San Luis Obispo   CA   93403

KCPR-md
Cal Poly State U
San Luis Obispo   CA   93407

KFSR-md
Cal. State
Shaw and Cedar Avenues
Fresno   CA   93740

KFCF-md
Box 4364
Fresno   CA   93744

KAZU-md
POB 206
Pacific Grove   CA   93950

KSPB-md
Robert Louis Stevenson
School
P.O. Box 657
Pebble Beach   CA 93953

KFJC-md
Foothill College
12345 El Monte
Los Altos Hills   CA 94022

KWST-md
POB 1799
Monterey   CA 93942

KITS-md
1355 Market St. #152
S.F.   CA 94103

KCSF-md
50 Phelan
S.F.   CA 94112

KUSF-md
University of San Francisco
2130 Fulton St.
S.F.   CA 94117

KSFS-md
S.F. State
1600 Holloway
S.F.   CA 94132

KMEL-md
55 San Francisco St. #400
S.F.   CA 94133

KZSU-md
Stanford Univ., Box B
Stanford   CA 94305

KVHS-md
1101 Alberta Way
Concord   CA 94521

KEGR-md
P.O. Box 103
Concord   CA 94522

KOHL-md
Ohlone College
Box 3909
Fremont   CA 94539

KCRH-md
25555 Hesperian Blvd.
Hayward   CA 94545

KVYN-md
1124 Foster Rd.
Napa   CA 94558

KSMC-md
St. Mary's College
Box 223
Moraga   CA 94575

KPFA-md
Box 288
Berkeley   CA 94701

KALX-md
UC Berkeley
2311 Bowditch
Berkeley   CA 94704

KSUN-md
Sonoma State University
1801 E. Cotati Ave
Rohnert Park   CA 94928

KZSC-md
UCSC
Santa Cruz   CA 95060

KSCU-md
University of Santa Clara
POB 1207
Santa Clara   CA 95053

KUSP-md
Box 423
Santa Cruz   CA 95060

KJCC-md
2100 Moorpark Ave.
San Jose   CA 95128

KSJS-md
San Jose State University
San Jose   CA 95192

KSJC-md
5151 Pacific Ave.
Stockton   CA 95207

KUOP-md
3601 Pacific Ave.
Stockton   CA 95211

KCSS-md
C.S.U. Stanislaus
801 W. Monte Vista Ave.
Turlock   CA 95380

KAFE-md
418 Mendecino Ave.
Santa Rosa   CA 95404

KVRE-md
Box 1712
Santa Rosa   CA 95402

KMLS-md
1275 4th St. #119
Santa Rosa   CA 95404

KHSU-md
Humboldt State Univ.
Arcata   CA 95521

KMUD-FM-md
POB 135
Redway   CA   95560

KDVS-md
UC Davis
14 Lower Freeborn
Davis   CA   95616

KCSC-md
Chico State University
POB 1580
Chico   CA   95927

KVMR-md
Box 1377
Nevada City   CA   95959

COLORADO

KBPI-md
1200 17th St.
1 Tabor Ctr. #2300
Denver   CO   80202

KRCX-md
5000 Lowell Blvd.
Denver   CO   80221

KAZY-md
2149 S. Holly St.
Denver   CO   80222

KBCO-md
4840 River Bend Rd.
Boulder   CO   80301

KGNU-md
Box 885
Boulder   CO   80306

KUCB-md
UC Campus Box 207
Boulder   CO   80307

KAIR-md
Univ. Memorial Center, 41-R
Box 207
Boulder   CO   80309

KFMU-md
2955 Village Drive
Steamboat Springs   CO
80467

KTCL-md
Box 2204
1608 Riverside Dr.
Fort Collins   CO   80522

KCSU-md
Colorado State University
Lory Student Center
Fort Collins   CO   80523

KSRR-md
Student Activities Area
Studio B
U. Northern Colorado
Greeley   CO 80639

KAFA-md
USAF Academy
P.O. Box 192
Colorado Springs   CO
80840

KRCC-md
117 Cache La Poudre St.
Colorado Springs   CO
80903

KEPC-md
5675 S. Academy Bl.
Warehouse B
Pikes Peak Comm. College
Colorado Springs   CO
80906

KASF-md
Adams State College
110 Richardson St.
Alamosa   CO 81102

KSUT-md
P.O. Box 737
Ignacio   CO 81137

KBUT-md
Box 308
Crested Butte   CO 81224

KWSB-md
Student Union
Western State College
Gunnison   CO 81230

KDUR-md
Fort Lewis College
Box 339
Durango   CO 81301

KOTO-FM
107 W. Columbia Ave.
Telluride   CO 81435

KMSA-md
Mesa State College
1175 Texas Ave.
Grand Junction   CO 81502

KSPN-md
P.O. Box 3317
Aspen   CO 81611

KZYR-md
Box 5559
Avon   CO 81620

KDNK-md
Box 1388
Carbondale   CO   81623

CONNECTICUT

WFCS-md
Certral Conn. State Univ.
1615 Stanley St.
New Britain   CT   06050

WRTC-md
Trinity College
Hartford   CT   06106

WSAM-md
University of Hartford
200 Bloomfield Ave.
West Hartford   CT   06117

WWUH-md
University of Hartford
200 Bloomfield Ave.
W. Hartford   CT   06117

WECS-md
Eastern Conn. State Univ.
83 Windham St.
Willimantic   CT   06226

WHUS-md
University of Connecticut
Box UBR 2110 Hillside Rd.
Storrs   CT   06268

WCNI-md
Connecticut College
Box 5333
New London   CT   06320

WVOF-md
Fairfield University
Fairfield   CT   06430

WMXC-md
Middlesex Community Coll.
100 Training Hill Rd.
Middletown   CT   06457

WESU-md
Wesleyan University
Box 2300, Wesleyan Sta.
Middletown   CT   06457

WMNR-md
1014 Monroe Tpk
Monroe   CT   06468

WSCB-md
Southern Conn. University
501 Crescent Ave.
New Haven   CT   06515

WNHU-md
University of New Haven
300 Orange Ave
West Haven   CT 06516

WQAQ-md
Quinnipiac College
555 New Rd.
Hamden   CT 06518

WYBC-md
Yale University
Box WYBC Yale Station
New Haven   CT 06520

WPKN-md
University of Bridgeport
244 Univ. Ave
Bridgeport   CT 06601

WSHU-md
SHU, Box 6460
Fairfield   CT 06606

WXCI-md
W. Connecticut State Coll.
181 White St.
Danbury   CT 06810

DELAWARE

WXDR-md
University of Delaware
Perkins Student Center
Newark   DE 19716

WDTS-md
Delaware Tech.
P.O.Box 610
Georgetown   DE 19947

FLORIDA

WFIN-md
Jacksonville University
Jacksonville   FL 32211

WVFS-md
Florida State University
420 Diffenbaugh
Tallahassee   FL 32306

WKGC-md
Gulf Coast Comm. College
5230 West Hwy 98
Panama City   FL 32401

WFSR-md
University of West Florida
Bldg. 22, Room 139
Pensacola   FL 32514

WRUF-md
Box 14444
University Station
Gainesville   FL   32604

WGVL
4908 NW 34th St.
Gainesville   FL   32605

WPRK-md
Rollins College
P.O. Box 2745
Winter Park   FL   32789

WUCF-md
University of Central Florida
P.O. Box 25000
Orlando   FL   32816

WFIT-md
Florida Institute of
Technology
150 W. University Blvd.
Melbourne   FL   32907

WVUM-md
University of Miami
Box 248191
Coral Gables   FL   33124

WLRN
172 NE 15th St.
Miami   FL   33132

WDNA-md
Box 8636
Miami   FL   33155

WMDS-md
Miami Dade Comm. College
11011 SW 104th St.
Miami   FL   33176

WUFI-md
Florida Int. University
University Park / UH 311
Miami   FL   33199

WNKR-md
Nova University
3301 College Ave.
Fort Lauderdale   FL   33314

WKPX-md
Piper High School
8000 NW 44th St.
Sunrise   FL   33351

WMNF-md
1210 E. Martin Luther King
Tampa   FL   33603

WBUL-md
University of South Florida
USF, AOC 216
Tampa   FL 33620

WECR-md
Eckerd College
Box W
St. Petersburg   FL 33733

WXTB-md
2 Corporate Dr. #550
Clearwater   FL 34622

GEORGIA

WGHR-md
Southern Tech.
1100 S. Marietta Pkwy.
Marietta   GA 30060

WWGC-md
West Georgia College
Box 10014
Carrolton   GA 30118

WRAS-md
Georgia State University
P.O. Box 4030
Atlanta   GA 30302

WMRE-md
Emory University
P.O. Box 21114
Atlanta   GA 30322

WREK
Georgia Tech.
Box 32743
Atlanta   GA 30332

WVGS-md
Georgia South. College
Landrum Box 11619
Statesboro   GA 30460

WUOG-md
University of Georgia
Box 2065 Memorial Hall
Athens   GA 30602

WXGC-md
Georgia College
Box 3124
Milledgville   GA 31061

WVVS-md
Valdosta State College /SUB
College Warehouse/
Pendleton
Valdosta   GA 31698

HAWAII

KAOI-md
1728C Kaahamanu Ave
Wailuku, Maui HI 96793

KTUH-md
University of Hawaii
2445 Campus Rd. #202
Honolulu HI 96822

IDAHO

KBSU-md
1910 University Dr.
Boise ID 83725

KUOI-md
University of Idaho
Student Union
Moscow ID 83843

ILLINOIS

WMWA-md
Glenbrook S. High
4000 West Lake Ave.
Glenview IL 60025

WVVX-md
210 Skokie Valley Rd.
Highland Park IL 60035

WMXM-md
Lake Forest College
Lake Forest IL 60045

WNTH-md
New Trier High School
385 Winnetka Ave.
Winnetka IL 60093

WKDI-FM/md
Northern Illinois University
544 College Ave.
Dekalb IL 60115

WRSE-md
Elmhurst College
190 Prospect Ave.
Elmhurst IL 60126

WGHS-md
430 Dorset Pl.
Glen Ellyn IL 60137

WRRG-md
Triton College
2000 5th Ave., Rm. 101A
River Grove IL 60171

WNUR-md
Northwestern University
1905 Sheridan Rd.
Evanston IL 60201

WCSF-AM/md
College of St. Francis
500 Wilcox St.
Joliet IL 60435

WLRA-md
Lewis University
Route 53
Romeoville IL 60441

WAAS-md
111th & Roberts Rd.
Palos Hills IL 60465

WARG-md
Argo High School
7329 W. 63rd St.
Summit IL 60501

WDGC-md
Downers Grove H.S.
4436 Main St.
Downers Grove IL 60515

WHSD-md
55th & Grand Streets
Hinsdale IL 60521

WLTL-md
Lyons Township High
100 S. Brainard Ave.
LaGrange IL 60525

WCRX-md
Columbia College
600 S. Michigan Ave.
Chicago IL 60605

WRDP-FM
DePaul University
2345 N. Clifton Ave.
Chicago IL 60614

WOUI-md
3300 South Federal St.
Chicago IL 60616

WYLL-md
2400 E. Devon Ave. #175
Des Plaines IL 60618

WZRD-md
5500 N. St. Louis Ave.
Chicago IL 60625

WHPK-md
University of Chicago
5706 S. University Ave.
Chicago IL 60637

WXRT
4949 W. Belmont
Chicago IL 60641

WXAV-md
St. Xavier College
3700 W. 103rd St.
Chicago IL 60643

WBSW-md
292 N. Convent
Bourbonnais IL 60915

WAUG-md
Augustana College
639 38th St.
Rock Island IL 61201

WVKC-md
Knox College
Box 154
Galesburg IL 61401

WIUS-md
Western Illinois University
432 Memorial
Macomb IL 61455

WMCR-md
Monmouth College
Monmouth IL 61462

WRBU-md
Bradley University
Peoria IL 61625

WESN-md
P.O. Box 2900
Illinois Wesleyan University
Bloomington IL 61701

KZND-md
Illinois State University
103 Media Center
Normal IL 61761

WRBA-md
1218 S. Main St.
Normal IL 61761

WEFT-md
113 N. Market
Champaign IL 61820

WPGU-md
204 East Peabody Dr.
Champaign IL 61820

WDBS-md
University of Illinois
204 East Peabody
Champaign IL 61820

WEIU-md
Radio/TV Center
Room 139
Eastern Illinois University
Charleston IL 61920

WSIE-md
Campus Box 1773
Edwardsville IL 62026

WTPC-md
Principia College
Elsah IL 62028

WLCA-md
5800 Godfrey Road
Lewis & Clark Community
College
Godfrey IL 62035

WMRY-md
9500 W. Illinois Rte. 15
Belleville IL 62223

WWQC-md
1800 College Avenue
Quincy College
Quincy IL 62301

WJMU-md
1184 West Main
Milikin University
Decatur IL 62522

WLNX-md
Lincoln College
300 Keokuk Street
Lincoln IL 62656

WVJC-md
2200 College Drive
Mt. Carmel IL 62863

WIDB-md
South Illinois University
Student Center 4th Floor
Carbondale IL 62901

INDIANA

WFCI-md
Franklin College
Journalism Department
Franklin IN 46131

WGRE-md
Student Union Building
Box 287
DePauw University
Greencastle IN 46135

WAJC-md
2835 North Illinois Street
Indianapolis IN 46208

WVUR-md
Valparaiso University
Box 31
Valparaiso   IN 46383

WVPE-md
2424 California Road
Elkhart   IN 46514

WSND-md
315 LaFortune Student Ctr.
Notre Dame University
Notre Dame   IN 46556

WVFI-md
315 La Fortune
Notre Dame University
Notre Dame   IN 46556

WEAX-md
West Park Street
Tri-State University
Angola   IN 46703

WCRD-md
Ball State University
Art & Communication Ctr.
2nd Floor
Muncie   IN 47306

WECI-md
Earlham College
Box E-1239
Richmond   IN 47374

WIUS-md
Indiana University
815 East 8th Street
Bloomington   IN 47401

WUEV-md
University of Evansville
1800 Lincoln Avenue
Evansville   IN 47722

WMHD-FM/md
Rose-Hulman Institute of
Technology
5500 Wabash Ave.
Terre Haute IN 47803

WCCR-md
Purdue University
Box M
Cary Quad
W. Lafayette   IN 47906

WLAY-md
Tarkington Hall
Purdue University
West Lafayette   IN 47906

WNDY-md
Wabash College
301 West Wabash
Crawfordsville   IN   47933

IOWA

KUSR-md
Iowa State University
1199 Friley Hall
Ames   IA   50012

KDIC-md
Grinnell College
Box V-4
Grinnell   IA   50112

KDRK-md
118 Meredith Hall
Drake University
Des Moines   IA   50311

KBLE-md
1170 22nd Street
Des Moines   IA   50311

KTPR-md
330 Avenue M
Fort Dodge   IA   50501

KUNI-md
University of Northern Iowa
Broadcasting Building
3rd Floor
Cedar Falls   IA   50614

KGRK-md
University of N. Illinois
Lower Level
Mackauer Union
Cedar Falls   IA   50614

KWAR-md
Wartburg College
Waverly   IA   50677

KLIF-md
3303 Rebecca Street
Sioux City   IA   51104

KLOR-md
Loras College
Box837
Dubuque   IA   52001

KWLC-md
700 College Drive
Luther College
Decorah   IA   52101

KRUI-md
University of Iowa
570 South Quad
Iowa City   IA 52242

KRNL-md
Cornell College
Commons Building
Mt. Vernon   IA 52314

KIGC-md
William Penn College
499 William Penn
Oskaloosa   IA 52577

KFMH-FM/md
3218 Mulberry Avenue
Muscataine   IA 52761

KALA-md
St. Ambrose College
Davenport   IA 52803

KANSAS

KNBU-md
Baker University
7th & Dearborn
Baldwin City   KS 66006

KJHK-md
200 Stauffer-Flint Hall
University of Kansas
Lawrence   KS 66045

KTJO-md
Ottawa University
Box10
Ottawa   KS 66067

KSDB-md
104 Kedzie Hall
Kansas State University
Manhattan   KS 66506

KMUW-md
3317 East 17th Street
Wichita State University
Wichita   KS 67208

KANZ-FM
Music Director
Pierceville   KS 67868

KENTUCKY

WFPL-md
301 York Street
Louisville   KY 40203

WLCV-md
Service Center
University of Louisville
Louisville   KY 40292

WRFL-md
University of Kentucky
Box777
University Station
Lexington   KY 40506

WNKU
Landrum Hall
N. Kentucky Univ.
Highland Hts.   KY 41076

WWHR-md
AC153 / Director of
Telecommunications
Western Kentucky University
Bowling Green   KY 42101

LOUISIANA

WTUL-md
Tulane University Center
New Orleans   LA 70118

WWNO-md
University of New Orleans
New Orleans   LA 70148

WWOZ-md
Box 51840
New Orleans   LA 70151

WHMD-md
200 E. Thomas Street
Box 1829
Hammond   LA 70403

KRVS-md
USL P.O. Box 42171
Lafayette   LA 70504

KLSU-md
B-39 Coates Hall
Louisiana State University
Baton Rouge   LA 70803

KNLU
N.E. Louisiana University
Monroe   LA 71201

KLPI-md
900 Gilman
Louisiana Tech.
Ruston   LA 71270

KNWD-md
Northwestern University
Box 3038
Nachitoches   LA 71457

MAINE

WBOR-md
c/o Moulton Union
Bowdoin College
Brunswick   ME 04011

WMPG-md
Univ. South. Maine
37 College Ave.
Gorham   ME 04038

WSJB-md
St. Joseph's College
No. Windham   ME 04011

WRBC-md
Bates College
Box 339
Lewiston   ME 04240

WMEB-md
University of Maine
106 E. Annex
Orono   ME 04469

WUPI -md
University of Maine
Box 64, Normal Hall
Presque Isle   ME 04769

WMHB-md
Colby College
Roberts Union
Waterville   ME 04901

WUMF-md
University of Maine
86 Main Street
Farmington   ME 04938

MARYLAND

WSMC-md
Saint Mary's College
St. Mary's City   MD 20686

WMUC-md
University of Maryland
Box 99
College Park   MD 20742

WHFS-md
8201 Corporate Dr.
Suite 550
Landover   MD 20785

WROC-md
Montgomery College
51 Mannakee St
Rockville   MD 20850

WTPK-md
Montgomery College
7600 New York Ave.
Tacoma Park   MD   20916

WHFC-md
Hartford Comm. College
401 Thomas Run Rd.
Bel Air   MD   21014

WCVT-md
Towson State University
Univ. Union Room 226
Towson   MD   21204

WBJC-md
2901 Liberty Heights
Baltimore   MD   21215

WJHU-md
34th & Charles Sts
Baltimore   MD   21218

WUMD-md
University of Maryland BC
5401 Wilkins Ave.
Catonsville   MD   21228

WBYQ-md
Essex Community College
7201 Rossville Bl.
Baltimore   MD   21237

WHFS-md
PO Box 29 / Admiral Dr.
Annapolis   MD   21404

WRNV-md
U.S. Naval Academy
Bancroft Hall
Annapolis   MD   21412

WFMW-md
Frostberg State University
P.O. Box 49 L. Center
Frostburg   MD   21532

WMTB-md
Box 1014
Mt. St. Mary's College
Emitsburg   MD   21727

WGTU-md
16315 Shinham Rd.
Hagerstown   MD   21740

WSUR-md
Salisbury State University
Box 3064
Salisbury   MD   21801

MASSACHUSETTS

WAMH - md
Amherst College
Box 1815 Station # 2
Amherst MA 01002

WMUA - md
102 Campus Center
University of MA
Amherst MA 01003

WOZQ-md
Smith College Radio Station
Northampton MA 01063

WMHC-md
Mount Holyoke College
South Hadley MA 01075

WSKB - md
Westfield State College
Ely Building
Westfield MA 01086

WTCC-md
Springfield Tech. C.C.
1 Armory Square
Springfield MA 01105

WNEK-FM
W. New England College
1215 Wilbraham Rd.
Sringfield MA 01119

WTBR-md
Valentine Rd.
Pittsfield MA 01201

WBEC
Box 958
Pittsfield MA 01202

WJJW - md
North Adams State College
Campus Center
North Adams MA 01247

WCFM - md
Baxter Hall
Williams College
Williamstown MA 01267

WRSI-md
P.O. Box 910
Green Field MA 01302

WGAJ-md
P.O. Box 248
Deerfield Academy
Deerfield MA 01342

WXPL - md
Fitchburg State College
160 Pearl St.
Fitchburg MA 01420

WSCW-md
Worcester State College
486 Chandler St.
Worcester MA 01602

WAAF-md
19 Norwich St.
Worcester MA 01608

WICN-md
6 Chatham St.
Worcester MA 01609

WACR-md
Assumption College
500 Salisbury St.
Worcester MA 01609

WCUW-md
910 Main St
Worcester MA 01610

WCHC-md
Holy Cross College
Box 35 A
Worcester MA 01610

WDJM-md
Framingham State College
College Center
100 State St.
Framingham MA 01701

WHAT-md
Bradford College
Route 125
Bradford MA 01835

WJUL - md
University of Lowell
1 University Ave
Lowell MA 01854

WFNX - md
25 Exchange St.
Lynn MA 01901

WMWM - md
Salem State College
352 Lafayette St.
Salem MA 01970

WBMT-md
R.F.D.
Topsfield MA 01983

WGAO-md
Dean Junior College
99 Main St.
Franklin MA 02038

WSFR-md
Suffolk University
41 Temple St.
Boston MA 02115

WRBB - md
Northeastern University
360 Huntington Ave.
Boston MA 02115

WERS-md
Emerson College
130 Beacon St.
Boston MA 02116

WECB-md
Emerson College
100 Beacon St.
Boston MA 02116

WUMB-md
U. Mass. Boston
Harbor Campus
Boston MA 02125

WHRB-md
Harvard University
45 Quincy St.
Cambridge MA 02138

WMBR-md
M.I.T.
3 Ames St
Cambridge MA 02142

WMFO - md
Tufts University
Box 65
Medford MA 02153

WBTY-md
Bentley College
Waltham MA 02154

WZBC-md
Boston College
McElroy Commons 107
Chestnut Hill MA 02167

WZLY-md
Wellesley College
Wellesley MA 02181

WMLN-md
Curry College
1071 Blue Hill Ave.
Milton MA 02186

WBCN-md
1265 Boylston St.
Boston MA 02215

WTBU - md
Boston University
640 Commonwealth Ave.
Boston MA 02215

WBRS- md
Brandeis University
415 South St.
Waltham MA 02254

WUSM-md
Old Westport Rd.
N Dartmouth MA 02254

WBIM-md
Bridgewater State College
Student Union Building
Bridgewater MA 02324

WSHL-md
Stonehill College
North Easton MA 02356

WKKL-md
Student Commons
Cape Cod Comm. College
W. Barnstable MA 02668

WSMU-md
Southeastern MA. University
Old Westport Rd.
N. Dartmouth MA 02747

WCCS-md
Wheaton College
P.O. Box 977
Norton MA 02766

MICHIGAN

WBFH-md
Andover High School
4200 Andover Rd.
Bloomfield Hills MI 48013

WOVI-md
Novi High School
24062 Taft Rd.
Novi MI 48050

WSGR-md
323 Erie St.
Port Huron MI 48060

WORW-md
1799 Kraft Rd.
Port Huron MI 48060

WPHS-md
30333 Hoover Rd.
Warren MI 48093

WCBN-md
University of Michigan
530 Student Activities Bldg.
Ann Arbor MI 48109

WHFR-md
Henry Ford College
5101 Evergreen
Dearborn   MI   48128

WUMD-md
University of Michigan
4901 Evergreen
Dearborn   MI   48128

WSDP-md
46181 Joy Rd.
Canton   MI   48187

WQBR-md
Eastern Michigan University
129 Quirk
Ypsilanti   MI   48197

WAYN-md
672 Putnam
Wayne State University
Detroit   MI   48202

WDET-FM
6001 Cass Ave.
Detroit   MI   48202

WTWR-md
University of Detroit
4001 W. McNichols - Box 91
Detroit   MI   48221

CIMX-md
Box 32576
Detroit   MI   48232

WOUX-md
69 Oakland Ctr.
Oakland University
Rochester   MI   48309

WORB-md
Oakland Community College
27055 Orchard Lake Rd.
Farmington   MI   48334

WFBE-md
605 Crapo
Flint   MI   48503

WLFT-md
Michigan State University
310 Auditorium Building
East Lansing   MI   48824

WDBM-md
Michigan State University
310 Auditorium Building
East Lansing   MI   48824

WMHW-md
Central Michigan University
180 Moore Hall
Mt. Pleasant   MI   48859

WLCC-md
P.O. Box 40010
430 North Capitol
Lansing MI 48901

WJMD-md
Kalamazoo College
1200 Academy St.
Kalamazoo MI 49007

WIDR-md
Western Michigan University
Student Services Building
Kalamazoo MI 49008

WASR-md
019A Campus Ctr.
Andrews University
Berrien Springs MI 49104

WVAC-md
Adrian College
110 S. Madison
Adrian MI 49221

WLBN-md
Albion College
S.C.&T. Center
Albion MI 49224

WRKX-md
Ferris State University
Patrick Building
Big Rapids MI 49307

WGVU-md
301 W. Fulton
Grand Rapids MI 49401

WTHS-md
Hope College
DeWitt Center
Holland MI 49423

WCAL-md
Calvin College
Grand Rapids MI 49506

WYCE-md
2820 Clyde Park Ave. SW
Wyoming MI 49509

WNMC-md
Northwestern Michigan
University
1701 E. Front
Traverse City MI 49684

WIMK-md
101 Kent St.
Iron Mountain MI 49801

WBKX-md
Northern Michigan
University
Marquette   MI 49855

WMTU-md
W. Wadsworth Hall
Michigan Tech.
Houghton   MI 49931

MINNESOTA

KRLX-md
Carleton College
Sayles Hill P.O.
Northfield   MN 55057

WMCN-md
Macalester College
1600 Grand Ave.
St. Paul   MN 55105

KABL-FM Cable/md
1363 Grand Ave.
St. Paul   MN 55105

KJJO-md
11320 Valley View Rd.
Minneapolis   MN 55344

KTCZ-md
100 N. 6th St.
Minneapolis   MN 55403

KFAI-md
1518 Lake St. 209
Minneapolis   MN 55407

WMMR-md
University of Minnesota
328 Coffman Union
300 Wash Ave. SE
Minneapolis   MN 55455

KUMD-md
University of Minnesota
Duluth   MN 55812

KRPR-md
Rochester Comm. College
851 30th Ave. SE
Rochester   MN 55904

KAVT-md
Austin Tech. Institute
1900 8th Ave. NW
Austin   MN 55912

KQAL-md
Winona State University
Performing Arts Ctr. 203
Winona   MN 55987

KSMR-md
St. Mary's College
Box 29
Winona   MN 55987

KRNR-md
Mankato State University
Box 46 Gage
Mankato   MN   56001

KXAX-md
P.O. Box 465
St. James   MN   56081

KUMM-md
University of Minnesota
Morris   MN   56267

KVSC-md
St. Cloud State University
27 Stewart Hall
St. Cloud   MN   56301

KSJU-md
St. John's University
Box 1255
Collegeville   MN   56321

WHMH-md
P.O. Box 366
Sauk Rapids   MN   56379

KORD-md
Concordia College
SCTA Department
P.O. Box 7
Moorhead   MN   56560

KDRS-md
1500 Birchmont Dr.
Bemidji   MN   56601

MISSISSIPPI

WMSU-md
University of So. Mississippi
Box 10045 Southern Station
Hattiesburg   MS   39406

WURC-md
Rust College
150 E. Rust Ave.
Holly Springs   MS   38635

WMUW-md
Division of Communication
P.O. Box W-940
Columbus   MS   39701

WMSB-md
PO Drawer PF
Mississippi State University
MS State   MS   39762

MISSOURI

KWMU-md
University of Missouri
580 Lucas Hall
St. Louis   MO   63121

KWUR-md
Box 1205
Washington University
St. Louis   MO 63130

KCFV-md
St. Louis Community College
3400 Pershall Rd.
St. Louis   MO 63135

KYMC-md
Maryville College
Box 622
Manchester   MO 63141

KDHX-md
P.O. Box 63328
St. Louis   MO 63163

KCLC-md
Lindenwood College
St. Charles   MO 63301

KNEU-md
A / H 105
Kirksville   MO 63501

KRC-md
5225 Troost Ave.
Kansas City   MO 64110

KDLX-md
Northwest Missouri State U.
Maryville   MO 64468

KOPN-md
915 E. Broadway
Columbia   MO 65201

KWWC-md
Stephens College
Box 2112
Columbia   MO 65201

KCOU-md
University of Missouri
101F Pershing Hall
Columbia   MO 65203

KNOS-md
Missouri Valley College
500 E. College St.
Marshall   MO 65340

KMNR-md
Box 203A Mining Bldg.
University of Missouri
Rolla   MO 65401

KORX-md
1915 S. Sagamont #12
Springfield   MO 65807

MONTANA

KGLT-md
Montana State University
Strand Union Bldg.
Bozeman   MT 59717

KUFM-md
University of Montana
Missoula   MT 59812

NEBRASKA

KBLZ-md
MBSC Room 128
506 N. 74th Ave.
Omaha   NE 68182

KZUM-md
941 'O' St., 10th Floor
Lincoln   NE 68508

KRNU-md
203 Avery Hall
University of Nebraska
Lincoln   NE 68588

KWSC-md
Wayne State College
Wayne   NE 68787

KSCV-md
Kearney State College
Michell Comm. Center
Kearney   NE 68849

NEVADA

KNPR -md
5151 Boulder Hwy.
Las Vegas   NV 89122

KUNV -md
University of Nevada
4505 Maryland Pkwy
Las Vegas   NV 89154

KUNR -md
University of Nevada
Reno NV 89507

NEW HAMPSHIRE

WNEC-md
New England College
Bridge Street
Henniker   NH 03242

WPCR-md
Plymouth State College
Silver Hall
Plymouth   NH 03264

WKNH-md
Keene State College
Elliot Hall
Keene   NH   03431

WMDK-md
PO Box 418
Peterborough   NH   03458

WFPR-MD
Franklin Pierce College
Basement of Library
Rindge   NH   03461

WDCR-md
Dartmouth College
Box 957
Hanover   NH   03755

WFRD-md
Dartmouth College
Box 957
Hanover   NH   03755

WHEB-md
Box 120
Lafayette Plaza
Portsmouth   NH   03801

WUNH -md
Memorial Union
Univ. of New Hampshire
Durham   NH   03824

WPEA-md
Phillips Exeter Academy
PEA Box 1000
Exeter   NH   03833

NEW JERSEY

WCPE-md
Union County College
1033 Springfield Ave.
Cranford   NJ   07016

WFMU-md
Upsala College
335 Prospect St.
East Orange   NJ   07019

WCPR-md
Box S-1461
Castle Point Station
Stevens Institute of Tech.
Hoboken   NJ   07030

WMSC-md
Montclair State College
Room 110, Student Center
Annex
Upper Montclair   NJ   07043

WSOU-md
Seton Hall University
400 S. Orange Ave.
South Orange   NJ   07079

WKNJ-md
Kean College
Morris Ave
Union   NJ   07083

WJTB-md
NJ Institute of Technology
323 High St.
Newark   NJ   07102

WRNU-md
Rutgers University
350 Martin Luther King Bl.
Newark   NJ   07102

WRPR-md
Ramapo State College
505 Ramapo Valley Rd.
Mahwah   NJ   07430

WCRN-md
William Patterson College
300 Pompton Rd.
Wayne   NJ   07470

WBCC-md
Bergen Community College
400 Paramus Rd.
Paramus   NJ   07652

WFDU-md
Fairleigh Dickinson
University
795 Cedar Ln.
Teaneck   NJ   07666

WHTG-FM /md
1129 Hope Rd.
Asbury Park   NJ   07712

WMCX-md
Monmouth College
Cedar & Norwood
W Long Branch NJ   07764

WNTI-md
Centenary College
400 Jefferson St.
Hackettstown   NJ   07840

WCCM-md
Center Grove Road
County College of Morris
Randolph   NJ   07869

WMNJ-md
Drew University
Madison   NJ   07904

WFDM-md
Fairleigh Dickinson
University
285 Madison Ave
Madison   NJ 07940

WJSV-md
50 Early St.
Morristown   NJ 07960

WDBK-md
Camden County College
PO Box 200
Blackwood   NJ 08012

WGLS-md
Glassboro State College
Glassboro   NJ 08028

WRBC-md
4th & Penn Streets
Camden NJ 08240

WMGM-md
15 S. Shore Rd.
Linwood   NJ 08221

WLFR-md
Stockton State College
Campus Activities
Pomona   NJ 08240

WPRB-md
Princeton University
Box 342
Princeton   NJ 08540

WRRC-md
Rider College
2083 Lawrenceville Rd.
Lawrenceville   NJ 08648

WTSR-md
Trenton State College
Brower Student Center
Trenton   NJ 08650

WOCC-md
Ocean County College
College Drive CN-2001
Toms River   NJ 08753

WRLC-md
Livingston College
Student Center Room 117
Piscataway   NJ 08854

WRSU-md
Rutgers University
126 College Ave
New Brunswick   NJ 08903

NEW MEXICO

KUNM -md
Campus & Girard NE
University of New Mexico
Albuquerque   NM   87131

KVNM -md
McArthy Plaza
Box 1844
Taos   NM   87571

KTAO-md
Blueberry Hill Rd.
Taos   NM   87571

KEDP-md
New Mexico Highlands
University
National Ave.
Las Vegas   NM   87701

KRUX -md
Box CC
New Mexico State University
Las Cruces   NM   88003

NEW YORK

WFIT-md
227 W.27th St.
Student Activities Rm. A-713
New York   NY   10001

WNYU-md
New York University
721 Broadway, 11th Floor
New York   NY   10003

WBMB-md
Baruch College
155 E. 24th St.
New York   NY   10010

WNEW-md
655 3rd Ave.
New York   NY   10017

WBAI-md
505 8th Ave
New York   NY   10018

WJJC-md
John Jay College of Criminal
Justice
445 W. 59th St.
New York   NY   10019

WHCS-md
Hunter College
695 Park Ave.
New York   NY 10021

WTNY-md
NY Inst. of Technology
1855 Broadway
New York   NY 10023

WKCR-md
Columbia University
208 Booth Hall
New York   NY 10027

WMOC-md
St. John's University
300 Howard Ave.
Staten Island   NY 10301

WSIA-md
College of Staten Island
715 Ocean Terrace
Staten Island   NY 10301

WFUV-md
Fordham University
Bronx NY 10458

WHLC-md
Lehman College
Bedford Park Blvd. W
Bronx NY 10468

WRCM-md
Box 85
Manhattan College
Bronx   NY 10471

WRPW-md
Pace University
861 Bedford Rd.
Pleasantville   NY 10570

WPUR-md
SUNY-Purchase
Purchase   NY 10577

WARY-md
Westchester Community
College
P.O. Box 258
Valhalla   NY 10595

WRTV-md
Iona College
1061 N. Broadway
Yonkers   NY 10701

WRTN-md
1 Broadcast Forum
New Rochelle   NY 10801

WICR-md
Iona College
715 North Avenue
New Rochelle   NY 10801

WRCC-md
Rockland Community Coll.
145 College Rd.
Suffern   NY 10901

WKDT-md
U.S. Military Academy
Building 720
West Point   NY 10996

WRBU-md
Box 734
USMMA
Kings Point   NY 11024

WNYE-md
112 Tillary St.
Brooklyn · NY 11201

WPIR-md
Pratt Institute
215 Willoughby Ave.
Box 117
Brooklyn   NY 11205

WHBI-md
477 82nd St
Brooklyn   NY 11209

WNWK
Box 115
Brooklyn   NY 11209

WBCR-md
Brooklyn College
Bedford & Ave. H
Brooklyn   NY 11210

WKRB-md
Kingsboro Community
College
2001 Oriental Blvd.
Brooklyn   NY 11235

WQCC-md
Queensborough Community
College
56th & Springfield
Batside   NY 11364

WSJU-md
St. John's University
Grand Central & Utopia
Jamaica   NY 11439

WBAU-md
Adelphi University
Box 365
Garden City   NY 11530

WCWP-md
CW Post College
Greenvale   NY 11548

WVHC-md
Hofstra University
Hempstead   NY 11550

WRHU-MD
Hofstra University
Hempstead   NY 11550

WNYT-md
268 Wheatley Rd.
Old Westbury   NY 11568

WDRE-md
1600 Stewart Ave.
Westbury   NY 11590

WBAB-md
555 Sunrise Hwy.
P.O. Box J
Babylon   NY 11704

WCTF-md
SUNY Farmingdale
Roosevelt Hall
Melville Rd.
Farmingdale   NY 11735

WHSE-md
Smithtown High School East
26 New York Ave.
St. James   NY 11780

WFTB-md
Five Towns College
2165 Seaford Ave.
Seaford   NY 11783

WKWZ-md
Syosset High School
Southwoods Rd.
Syosset   NY 11791

WUSB-md
SUNY at Stonybrook
Student Union
Stonybrook   NY 11794

WPOB-md
Plainview Old Bethpage
Central School District
50 Kennedy Dr.
Plainview   NY 11803

WRPI-md
Rensselaer Polytechnic
Institute
1 WRPI Plaza
Troy   NY 12180

WQBK-FM/md
Box 1300
Albany   NY 12201

WTSC-md
Clarkson University
Potsdam   NY 12208

WCDB-md
SUNY at Albany
Campus Center 316
1400 Washington Ave.
Albany   NY 12222

WRUC-md
Carnegie Hall
Union College
Schenectady   NY 12308

WDST-md
118 Tinker St.
Woodstock   NY 12498

WFNP-md
SUNY at New Paltz
Sub 413
New Paltz   NY 12561

WDCC-md
Duchess Community Coll.
Pendall Road
Poughkeepsie   NY 12601

WMCR-md
Marist College
290 North Road
Poughkeepsie   NY 12601

WVKR-md
Box 166
Vassar College
Poughkeepsie   NY 12601

WSPN-md
Skidmore College
Saratoga Springs   NY 12866

WPLT-md
SUNY at Plattsburg
Angell College Center 110
Plattsburgh   NY 12901

WDWN-md
Franklin St.
Cayuga Community College
Auburn   NY 13021

WITC-md
Cazenovia College
Cazenovia   NY 13035

WSUC-md
SUNY at Cortland
Brockway Hall
Cortland   NY 13045

WOCR-md
Oswego State University
Hewitt Union
Oswego   NY 13126

WSFW-md
1 Water St.
Seneca Falls   NY 13148

WERW-md
Syracuse University
Schine Student Center 105
303 University Place
Syracuse   NY 13244

WAER-md
215 University Pl.
Syracuse   NY 13244

WHCL-md
Hamilton College
Clinton   NY 13323

WRCU-md
Colgate University
Hamilton   NY 13346

WHCR-md
Herkimer Community
College
Reservoir Rd.
Herkimer   NY 13350

WPNR-md
Faculty Box 239
Utica College
Utica   NY 13502

WOUR-md
288 Genessee St.
Utica   NY 13502

WCOT-md
SUNY College of Technology
P.O. Box 3030
Utica   NY 13504

WONY-md
Oneonta State College
Alumni Hall
Oneonta   NY 13820

WRHO-md
Hartwick College
Oneonta   NY 13820

WHRW-md
SUNY at Binghampton
University Union
Binghampton   NY 13901

WGCC-md
1 College Rd.
Batavia   NY 14020

WCVF-md
109 Gregory Hall
SUNY at Fredonia
Fredonia   NY 14063

WRNU-md
Alumni Hall
Niagra University
Niagra   NY   14109

WNCB-md
Niagra County Community
College
3111 Saunders Settlement Rd
Sanborn   NY   14132

WXBX-md
425 Franklin St.
Buffalo   NY   14202

WUWU-md
6 Fountain Plaza
Buffalo   NY   14202

WBFO-md
3435 Main St
Buffalo   NY   14214

WECC-md
Erie Community College
North Campus
Main St and Young Rd
Williamsville   NY   14221

WBNY-md
Buffalo State College
1300 Elmwood Ave
Buffalo   NY   14222

WRUB-md
SUNY/Buffalo
174 MFAC
Amherst   NY   14261

WBSU-md
Seymour College Union
SUNY Brockport
Brockport   NY   14420

WGSU-md
Fraser Mailroom
SUNY at Geneseo
Geneseo   NY   14454

WEOS-md
Box F-138
Hobart College
Geneva   NY   14456

WBER-FM-md
2596 Baird Rd.
Penfield   NY   14526

WIRQ-md
260 Cooper Rd.
Irondequoit High School
Rochester   NY   14617

WMCC-md
1000 E. Henrietta Rd.
Monroe Community College
Rochester   NY   14623

WITR-md
Rochester Institute of Tech.
Box 9969
Rochester   NY 14623

WRUR-md
University of Rochester
Box 277356
Rochester   NY 14627

WSBU-md
Drawer o
St. Bonaventure   NY 14778

WETD-md
Orvis Activities Center
Alfred State College
Alfred   NY 14802

WALF-md
PO Box 548
Alfred University
Alfred   NY 14802

WCEB-md
Corning College
Commons Building Box 200
Corning   NY 14830

106 VIC-md
Hanna Broadcast Center
Ithica College
Ithica   NY 14850

WVBR-md
Cornell University
227 Linden Av.
Ithica   NY 14850

WICB-md
Ithica College
Dillingham Ctr.
Ithica   NY 14850

WNGZ-md
421 N. Franklin St.
Watkins Glen   NY 14891

NORTH CAROLINA

WAKE-md
Wake Forest University
Box 7760 Reynolds Station
Winston-Salem   NC 27109

WSOE-md
Elon College
Box 6000
Elon College   NC 27244

WWIH-md
P.O. Box 3071 HP-2
High Point   NC 27261

WQFS-md
Guilford College
Founders Hall
Greensboro   NC   27412

WUAG-md
UNC Greensboro
Taylor Building UNCG 6
Greensboro   NC   27412

WQFS-md
5800 W. Friendly Ave.
Greensboro   NC   27403

WXYC-md
University of North Carolina
Box 51 Carolina Union
Chapel Hill   NC   27599

WKNC-md
P.O. Box 8607
N. Carolina State University
Raleigh   NC   27695

WXDU-md
Duke University
P.O. Box 4706
Duke Station
Durham   NC   27706

WZMB-md
East Carolina University
Old Joyner Library
Second Floor
Greenville   NC   27834

WDAV-md
PO Box 1540
Davidson   NC   28036

WNCW-md
P.O.Box 804
Spindale   NC   28160

WUAW-md
Route 1 Box 210
Erwin   NC   28339

WSAP-md
St. Andrews Presb. College
1700 Dogwood Mile
Larinburg   NC   28352

WLOZ-md
UNC Wilmington
601 S. College Rd.
Wilmington   NC   28403

WXCR-md
P.O. Box 938
Hickory   NC   28603

WLRC-md
Lenoir-Rhyne College
P.O.Box 7164
Hickory   NC 28603

WASU-md
Wey Hall
Appalachian State Univ.
Boone   NC 28608

WWCU-md
414 Helder Hall
Cullowhee   NC 28723

WVMH-md
P.O.Box 1161-C
Mars Hill   NC 28754

WUNF-md
Univ. of North Carolina
Ashville   NC 28804

WCQS-md
One Univ. Heights
Ashville   NC 28804

NORTH DAKOTA

KDSU-md
Ceres Hall
N. Dakota State University
Fargo   ND 58105

KXUM-md
University of Mary
7500 University Dr.
Bismark   ND 58504

KMSU-md
Minot State University
500 West University
Minot   ND 58701

OHIO

WSLN-md
Ohio Wesleyan University
Delaware   OH 43015

WKCO-md
Kenyon College
P.O. Box 312
Gambier   OH 43022

WDUB-md
Denison University
Granville   OH 43023

WOSR-md
Ohio State University
Ohio Union Suite 15R
1739 N. High St.
Columbus   OH 43210

WQSR-md
1849 Cannon Dr.
Columbus   OH   43210

WBGU-md
Bowling Green State Univ.
413 West Hall
Bowling Green   OH   43403

WFAL-md
Bowling Green State Univ.
Bowling Green   OH   43403

WXUT-md
University of Toledo
2801 West Bancroft
Toledo   OH   43606

WMCO-md
Muskingum College
New Concord   OH   43762

WBWC-md
Baldwin-Wallace College
Berea   OH   44017

WKHR-md
17425 Snyder Rd.
Chagrin Falls   OH   44022

WTLS-md
Lakeland College
I-90 and Route 306
Mentor   OH   44060

WOBC-md
Oberlin College
Wilder Hall
Oberlin   OH   44074

WRUW-md
Case Western Reserve
11220 Bellflower Rd.
Cleveland   OH   44106

WMMS-md
1200 Statler Office Tower
Cleveland   OH   44115

WCSB-md
Cleveland State University
1983 East 24th St.
Room 956 Rhodes Tower
Cleveland   OH   44115

WUJC-md
John Carroll University
20700 N. Park Blvd.
Univ. Heights   OH   44118

WHHS-md
5947 Ogilby Dr.
Hudson   OH   44236

WKSR-md
519 Wright Hall
Kent State University
Kent OH 44242

WRHA-md
265 E. Buchtel Ave.
Akron OH 44304

WAPS-md
Akron Board of Eduction
70 North Broadway
Akron OH 44308

WONE-md
853 Copley Rd.
Akron OH 44320

WZIP-md
University of Akron
Akron OH 44325

WCWS-md
The College of Wooster
Wishart Hall
Wooster OH 44691

WRDL-md
Ashland College
401 College Ave.
Ashland OH 44805

WCPZ-md
Box 1390
105 West Market
Sandustky OH 44870

WHEI-md
Founders Hall
Heidelberg College
Tiffin OH 44883

WMSR-md
Miami University
Williams Hall
Oxford OH 45056

WOXY-md
5120 College Corner Pike
Oxford OH 45056

WAIF-md
2525 Victory Pkwy.
Cincinnati OH 45206

WVXU-md
Xavier University
3800 Victory Pkwy.
Cincinnati OH 45207

WGUC-md
1223 Central Pkwy.
Cincinnati OH 45214

WTUE-md
11 S. Wilkinson St.
Dayton   OH   45402

WDPS-md
Dayton Public Schools
441 River Corridor Dr.
Dayton   OH   45402

WYSO-FM/md
Box 166
Wright Bros. Station
Dayton   OH   45409

WKET-md
Fairmont High School
3301 Shroyer Rd.
Kettering   OH   45429

WWSU-md
Wright State University
44 University Center
Col. Glenn Hwy.
Dayton   OH   45435

WUSO-md
Wittenburg University
Box 720
Springfield   OH   45501

WLHD-md
Ohio University
South Green Office
Athens   OH   45701

WXTQ-md
300 N. Columbus Rd.
Athens   OH   45701

WSGR-md
Ohio University
S. Green Office
Athens   OH   45701

ACRN-md
Suite 315 R-TV Building
Athens   OH   45701

WHMQ-md
101 W. Sandusky St.
Findlay   OH   45840

OKLAHOMA

KBLZ-md
Central State University
Edmond   OK   73013

KGOU-md
University of Oklahoma
780 Van Fleet Oval
Norman   OK   73019

KTOW-md
8886 W. 21
Sand Springs   OK 74063

KOSU-md
Oklahoma State University
302 Paul Miller
Stillwater   OK 74078

KHIB-md
Southeast Oklahoma Univ.
Comm. Department Sta. A
Durant   OK 74701

OREGON

KMUN-md
Box 269
Astoria   OR 97103

KPUR-md
Pacific University
2043 College Way
Forest Grove   OR 97116

KSLC-md
Box 365
Linfield College
McMinnville   OR 97128

KRRC-md
Reed College
Portland   OR 97202

KDUP-md
University of Portland
5000 N. Williamette Bl.
Portland   OR 97203

KBOO-md
20 SE 8th Ave.
Portland   OR 97214

KOAP-md
7140 SW Macalam Ave.
Portland   OR 97219

KLC-md
Lewis & Clark University
Portland   OR 97219

KWU-md
Williamette University
900 State St. D-237
Salem   OR 97301

KBVR-md
Memorial Union East
Oregon State University
Corvallis   OR 97331

KRXX-md
1430 Williamette #315
Eugene   OR 97401

KRVM-md
200 N. Monroe St.
Eugene   OR 97402

KLCC-md
4000 E. 30 th Ave.
Eugene   OR 97405

KZAM-md
105 West "Q" Street
Springfield   OR 97477

KTEC-md
Oregon Institute of Tech.
3201 Campus Dr.
Klamath Falls   OR 97601

KEOL-md
Eastern Oregon State Coll.
1410 L Ave.
La Grande   OR 97850

PENNSYLVANIA

WXVX-md
1 Progressive Alley
Monroeville   PA 15146

WRCT-md
Carnegie-Mellon University
5020 Forbes Ave
Skibo Hall
Pittsburgh   PA 15213

WDSR-md
Duquesne Student Radio
SMC 2500
1345 Vickroy St.
Pittsburgh   PA 15219

WPPJ-md
Box 626
201 Wood Street
Pittsburgh   PA 15222

WYEP-md
Box #66 Woodland Rd
Pittsburgh   PA 15232

WPTS-md
University of Pittsburgh
Box 411
William Pitt Union
Pittsburgh   PA 15260

WVCS-md
California University of
Pittsburgh
428 Hickory St.
California   PA 15419

WIUP-md
Indiana Univ. of Penn.
121 Stouffer Hall
Indiana   PA   15705

WGLU-md
516 Main St.
Johnstown   PA   15901

WUPJ-md
University of Pittsburgh
140 Biddle Hall
Johnstown   PA   15904

WSRU-md
Slippery Rock University
223 ECB-WSRU
Slippery Rock   PA   16057

WRCK-md
Slippery Rock University
C211 University Union
Slippery Rock   PA   16057

WTGP-md
Thiel College
College Ave.
Greenville   PA   16125

WCCB-md
Clarion University
102 Harvey Hall
Clarion   PA   16214

WARC-md
Box C
Alleghaney College
Meadville   PA   16335

WFSE-md
Room 102 Compton Hall
Edinboro College
Edinboro   PA   16444

WERG-md
Gannon University
Erie   PA   16541

WMCY-md
Mercyhurst College
Glenwood Hills
Erie   PA   16546

WFBG-md
P.O.Box 2005
Hilltop Logan Blvd.
Altoona   PA   16603

WKVR-md
Juanita College
Box 1005
Huntingdon   PA   16652

WPSU-md
Penn State University
304 Sparks Bldg.
University Park   PA   16802

WERH-md
104 Johnston Hall
University Park   PA   16802

WXMU-md
Mansfield University
Box 84 South Hall
Mansfield   PA   16933

WDCV-md
Dickinson College
Carlisle   PA   17013

WTPA-md
970 West Trindle Rd.
Mechanicsburg   PA   17055

WPSH-md
Penn State University
Middletown   PA   17057

WZBT-md
Box 435
Gettysburg College
Gettysburg   PA   17325

WVYC-md
York College
Country Club Rd.
York   PA   17405

WIXQ-md
Millersville University
Millersville   PA   17551

WFNM-md
Franklin & Marshall College
Box 3003
Lancaster   PA   17604

WRLC-md
Lycoming College
Williamsport   PA   17701

WWAS-md
Pennsylvania College of
Technology
1 College Ave
Williamsport   PA   17701

WLHU-md
710 Robinson Hall
Lock Haven   PA   17701

KTTZ-md
738 Bellefonte Ave.
Lock Haven   PA   17745

WVBU-md
Bucknell University
Box 3088
Lewisburg   PA   17837

WQSU-md
Susquehanna University
Selinsgrove   PA 17870

WLVR-md
Lehigh University
Box 20A
Bethlehem   PA 18015

WNCC-md
Northampton Community
College
3835 Green Pond Rd
Bethlehem   PA 18017

WRMC-md
Moravian College
Box 2
Bethlehem   PA 18017

WJRH-md
Box 4029
Lafayette College
Easton   PA 18042

WXLV-md
Lehigh County Community
College
2370 Main St.
Schnecksville   PA 18078

WMUH-md
Box 2806
Muhlenberg College
Allentown   PA 18104

WESS-md
198 Student Center
E. Stroudsburg University
E. Stroudsburg   PA 18301

WVMW-md
Marywood College
Scranton   PA 18509

WYRE-md
University of Scranton
Scranton   PA 18510

WSFX-md
Luzerne County Community
College
Prospect St. & Middle Rd.
Nanticoke   PA 18634

WVIA-md
Old Boston Rd.
Pittston   PA 18640

WRKC-md
King's College
Wilkes Barre   PA 18711

WCLH-md
Speech Department
Wilkes College
Wilkes-Barre   PA   18766

WRDV-md
Box 2012
Warminster   PA   18974

WRFT-md
Temple University
Meetinghouse Rd.
Ambler   PA   19002

WIOQ-md
2 Bala Cynwyd Plaza
Bala Cynwyd   PA   19004

WDNR-md
Box 1000
Widener University
Chester   PA   19013

WBVR-md
Beaver College
Glenside   PA   19038

WHRC-md
Haverford College
Haverford   PA   19041

WDCR-md
Delaware County Commu-
nity College
Media   PA   19038

WSRN-md
Swarthmore College
Swarthmore   PA   19081

WHHS-md
200 Mill Rd.
Haverford High School
Havertown   PA   19083

WKVU-md
Box 105 Tollintine Hall
Villanova University
Villanova   PA   19085

WCAB-md
Cabrini College
Eagle and King of Prussia
Radnor   PA   19087

WMMR-md
19th & Walnut St.
Philadelphia   PA   19103

WKDU-md
Drexel University
3210 Chestnut St.
Philadelphia   PA   19104

WXPN-md
University of Pennsylvania
3905 Spruce St
Philadelphia   PA   19104

WQHS-md
University of Philadelphia
3905 Spruce St.
Philadelphia   PA   19104

WHYY-FM/md
150 N. 6th St.
Philadelphia   PA   19106

WSJR-md
5600 City Avenue
Philadelphia   PA   19131

WEXP-md
LaSalle University
20th & Olney Ave.
Philadelphia   PA   19141

WZZE-md
Glen Mills Schools
Concordville   PA   19331

WCUR-md
West Chester University
219 Sykes Union Building
West Chester   PA   19383

WRFM-md
Montgomery County
Community College
340 Dekalb Pike
Blue Bell   PA   19422

WVOU-md
Ursinus College
Collegevilel   PA   19426

WRKU-md
Kutztown College
Rothermel Hall Down Under
Kutztown   PA   19530

WXAC-md
PO Box 15234
Albright College
Reading   PA   19612

RHODE ISLAND

WQRI-md
Roger Williams College
Bristol   RI   02809

WJHD-md
Portsmouth Abbey School
Portsmouth   RI   02871

WRIU-md
University of Rhode Island
362 Memorial Union
Kingston RI 02881

WXIN
Rhode Island College
600 Mt. Pleasant Ave.
Providence RI 02908

WBRU-md
Brown University
88 Benevolent St.
Providence RI 02906

WELR-md
The Wheeler School
216 Hope St.
Providence RI 02906

WHJY-md
115 Eastern Ave.
E. Providence RI 02914

WJMF-md
Bryant College
PO Box 6
Smithfield RI 02917

WDOM-md
Friar Box 377
Providence College
Providence RI 02918

SOUTH CAROLINA

WUSC-md
University of S. Carolina
Drawer B
Columbia SC 29208

WPLS-md
Furman Univ.
Box 28573
Greenville SC 29613

WSBF-md
Clemson University
Box 2156 University Station
Clemson SC 29631

SOUTH DAKOTA

KESD-md
S. Dakota State University
Brookings SD 57006

KAOR-md
University of S. Dakota
Mass Communications Dept.
Vermillion SD 57069

KCFS-md
Sioux Falls College
1501 S. Prarie
Sioux Falls SD 57105

KAUR-md
28th & Summit
Augustana College
Sioux Falls   SD 57102

KASD-md
Northern State College
Aberdeen   SD 57401

KTEQ-md
S. Dakota School of Mines
500 E. St. Joe
Rapid City   SD 57701

KBHU-md
1200 University Ave.
Box 9665 College Station
Spearfish   SD 57783

TENNESSEE

WRLT-md
215 Centerview Dr. #351
Brentwood   TN 37027

WRVU-md
Vanderbilt University
Box 6303 Station B
Nashville   TN 37235

WUTS-md
Univ. of the South
Student Post Office
Sewanee   TN 37375

WAWL-md
Chattanooga St. Tech.
Chattanooga   TN 37406

WUOT-md
University of Tennessee
232 Comm. Building
Knoxville   TN 37916

WUTK-md
Univ. of Tennessee
P103 Andy Holt Tower
Knoxville   TN 37996

WEVL-md
518 Main St
Memphis   TN 38103

WLYX-FM
Rhodes College
2000 N. Parkway
Memphis   TN 38112

WFHC-md
Freed-Hardeman College
158 E. Main St.
Henderson   TN 38340

WUTZ
156 Drakes Ln.
Summertown   TN 38483

WTTU-md
Tennessee Tech.
Box 5113
Cookeville   TN 38505

TEXAS

KDGE-md
700 Courtyard Tower
1320 Greenway Dr.
Irving   TX 75038

KERA-md
3000 Harry Hines Blvd.
Dallas   TX 75201

KZEW-md
Communications Center
Dallas   TX 75202

KSMU-md
Box 400
Southern Methodist Univ.
Dallas   TX 75275

KWBU-md
Baylor University
Castellaw Comm. Center
Waco   TX 76798

KTSU-md
3101 Wheeler Ave.
Houston   TX 77004

KPFT-md
419 Lovett Blvd.
Houston   TX 77006

KTRU-md
Rice University
Box 1892
Houston   TX 77251

KSHU-md
Sam Houston State Univ.
Box 2207
Huntsville   TX 77341

KANM-md
Texas A&M University
P.O. Box 377
College Station   TX 77841

KSYM-md
San Antonio College
1300 San Pedro Ave.
San Antonio   TX 78284

KNCN-md
Box 9781
5544 Leopard
Corpus Christi   TX 78469

KAT-md
Southwest Texas State Univ.
San Marcos   TX 78666

KUT-md
University of Texas
Center for Telecomm.
Austin   TX 78712

KTSB Radio-md
University of Texas
P.O. Box D
Austin   TX 78713

KATP-md
3500 140 E.
Box 30000
Amarillo   TX 79120

KTXT-md
Box 4170 Tech Station
Lubbock   TX 79409

KXCR-md
2023 Myrtle St.
El Paso   TX 79901

KTEP-md
University of Texas, El Paso
El Paso   TX 79968

KVOF-md
University of Texas, El Paso
El Paso   TX 79968

UTAH

KCGL-md
481 S. Orchard Dr.
Bountiful   UT 84010

KRCL -md
208 W 800 South
SLC   UT 84101

KUTE -md
University of Utah
Salt Lake City   UT 84112

KUSU -md
Utah State University
Logan   UT 84322

KWCR -md
3750 Harrison Blvd.
Ogden   UT 84408

KBYU -md
Brigham Young University
C-302 HFAC
Provo   UT 84602

KCDR -md
Southern Utah State College
Cedar City   UT 84720

VERMONT

WEQX-md
Elm St. and Highland Ave.
Manchester VT 05254

WWPV-md
Saint Michael's College
Winooski
Winooski   VT   05404

WRUV-md
University of Vermont
Billings Student Center
Burlington   VT 05405

WIZN- md
The Stevens House
Vergennes VT 05491

WNCS-md
7 Main St.
Montpelier   VT 05602

WJSC-md
Johnson State College
Box A-37
Johnson   VT 05656

WNUB-md
Norwich University
Webb Hall
Northfield   VT 05663

WGDR-md
Goddard College
Plainfield   VT 05667

WRFB-md
Box 26
Stowe   VT 05672

WIUV-md
Campus Center
Castleton State College
Castleton   VT 05735

WRMC-md
Drawer 29
Middlebury College
Middlebury   VT 05753

WWLR-md
Lyndon State College
Box F
Lyndonville   VT 05851

VIRGINIA

WGMU-md
George Mason University
4400 University Drive
Fairfax   VA 22030

WMWC-md
Mary Washington College
Fredricksburg   VA 22401

WXJM-md
P.O.Box l-247
James Madison University
Harrisonburg   VA 22807

WGMB-md
BC P.O. Box 132
Bridgewater   VA 22812

WTJU-md
Thomas Jefferson University
Box 711, Newcombe Station
Charlottesville   VA 22901

WIRE-md
University of Virginia
P.O. Box 531
Newcomb Hall Station
Charlottesville   VA 22904

WDCE-md
Box 85
University of Richmond
Richmond   VA 23284

WCWM-md
College of William & Mary
Williamsburg   VA 23185

WVCW-md
Student Commons Box 2032
907 Floyd Ave.
Richmond   VA 23284

WTZR-md
P.O. Box 16236
Chesapeake   VA 23328

WHOV-md
Hampton Institute
Hampton   VA 23368

WVAW-md
Virginia Wesleyan College
Wesleyan Drive
Norfolk   VA 23502

WODU-md
Old Domion University
Room 201 Web Center
Norfolk   VA 23508

WLCX-md
Longwood College
Dept. of Speech & Theatre
Farmville   VA 23901

WWHS-md
P.O.Box 606
Hampden-Sydney College
Hampden-Sydney   VA
23943

WUVT FM-md
Virginia Tech.
352 Squires Student Ctr.
Blacksburg   VA 24061

WVVV-md
1780 N. Franklin St.
Christianburg   VA 24073

WFFC-md
Ferrum College
Ferrum   VA 24088

WLUR-md
Wash & Lee University
Lexington   VA 24450

WWLC-md
Box 9271
Lynchburg College
Lynchburg   VA 24501

WASHINGTON

KGRG-md
Green River Community
College
12401 SE 320th St.
Auburn   WA 98002

KASB-md
601 108th Ave. SE
Bellvue   WA 98004

KBCS-md
Bellvue Comm. College
Box 92700
Bellevue   WA 98009

KEZX-md
3876 Bridge Way N.
Seattle   WA 98103

KISW-md
P.O.Box 21449
Seattle   WA 98111

KJET-md
200 W Mercer #304
Seattle   WA 98119

KRAB-md
2212 S. Jackson
Seattle   WA 98144

KCMU-md
304 Comm. DS-55
University of Washington
Seattle   WA 98195

KUGS-md
W. Washington University
410 Viking Union
Bellingham   WA 98225

KTPS-md
1101 S. Yakima Ave.
Tacoma   WA 98405

KUPS-md
University of Puget Sound
Room 1 Sub
Tacoma   WA 98416

KCCR-md
Pacific Lutheran University
Tacoma   WA 98447

KAOS-md
TESC
Olympia   WA 98505

KCWS-md
Central Wash. State College
Ellensburg   WA 98926

KEWU-md
Eastern Washington Univ.
MS 105
Cheney   WA 99004

KZUU-md
Washington State University
WilsonCompton Union Bldg.
3rd Floor
Pullman   WA 99163

KWRS-md
Whitworth College
Spokane   WA 99218

KAGU-md
Gonzaga University
Spokane   WA 99258

KWCW-md
Whitman College
Walla Walla   WA 99362

WASHINGTON D.C.

WETA-md
Box 2626
Washington   DC 20013

WVAU-MD
American University
610 Eagle Station
Washington   DC   20016

National Public Radio
Performance Today
2025 M Street NW
Washington   DC   20036

National Public Radio
All Things Considered
2025 M Street NW
Washington   DC   20036

WHFS -md
c/o Circle Theaters
1101 23rd St. NW
Washington   DC   20037

WRGW-md
800 21st St. NW
Marvin Center Room 428
Washington   DC   20052

WGTB-md
Georgetown University
316 Leavey Center
Washington   DC   20057

WCUA-md
Box 184 Cardinal Station
Catholic University
Washington   DC   20064

WISCONSIN

WBSD-md
Burlington High School
225 Robert St.
Burlington   WI   53105

WZRX-md
University of Wisconsin
Box 2000 Wood Road
Kenosha   WI   53141

KBLE-md
Gateway Tech. Institute
3520 30th Ave. Box 1486
Kenosha   WI   53144

WYRE-md
University of Wisconsin
1500 University Dr.
Waukesha   WI   53186

WCCX-md
100 N.E. Ave.
Waukesha   WI   53186

WSUW-md
University of Wisconsin
301 Hyer Hall
Whitewater   WI   53190

WMSE-md
Milwaukee School of Eng.
1025N. Milwaukee St.
Room C-24
Milwaukee   WI   53201

WUWM-md
University of Wisconsin
Milwaukee   WI   53201

WTPS-md
Box 92871
Milwaukee   WI   53202

WLUM-md
2500 N. Mayfair Rd. #390
Milwaukee   WI   53226

WMUR-md
Marquette University
College of Speech
Milwaukee   WI   53233

WBCR-md
Beloit College
Beloit   WI   53511

WORT-md
118 S. Bedford St.
Madison   WI   53703

WLHA-md
Holt Commons
University of Wisconsin
Madison   WI   53706

WSUP-md
42 Pioneer Tower
1 University Tower
Platteville   WI   53818

WSNC-md
St. Norberts College
DePre   WI   54115

WGBW-md
University of Wisconsin
2420 Nicolet Dr.
Green Bay   WI   54301

WWSP-md
University of Wisconsin
101 Communications Bldg.
Stevens Point   WI   54481

KUWS-md
University of Wisconsin
1800 Grand Ave.
Superior   WI   54880

WRST-md
University of Wisconsin
800 Algoma Blvd.
Oshkosh   WI 54901

WLFM-md
113 S. Lawe St.
Appleton   WI 54911

WAPL-md
P.O. Box 1519
Appleton   WI 54913

WRPN-md
Ripon College
Ripon   WI 54971

WEST VIRGINIA

WCCR-md
Division of Fine Arts Box 63
Concord College
Athens   WV 24712

WMUL-md
Marshall University
400 Hal Greer Blvd.
Huntington   WV 25755

WVBC-md
Bethany College
Bethany   WV 26032

WCDE-md
Davis & Elkins College
Box J
Elkins   WV 26241

WWVU-md
West Virginia University
Mountainclair WVU
Morgantown   WV 26506

WTCS-md
PO Box 1549
Fairmont   WV 26555

WYOMING

KUWR-md
Univ. of Wyoming
P.O. Box 3984
Laramie   WY 82070

KRQU-md
409 S. 4th St.
Box 818
Laramie   WY 82070

KCWC-md
Central Wyoming College
2660 Peck Ave.
Riverton   WY 82501

Conclusion

By now, you've probably figured out that getting your music played on radio isn't as easy as you might have thought. It's definitely hard work. The priciples and ideas in this book are the *reality* side of the music industry, not the fantasy MTV mega-star side. But, if you show me 99% of the successful, major music acts today, I'll show you the independently produced and promoted first album they put out a few years ago. Getting radio airplay (or success in the music industry, for that matter) is not a simple, one-shot, affair. You need to build up a rapport with the stations, fans, and clubs over the course of several releases. No, it's not easy, but yes, it's worth it. If new, innovative artists don't take it upon themselves to get their music to the masses, then music is dead. Hopefully, this book can help you acheive your goals.
Support independent music.

Comments, questions and letters to Gary Hustwit should be mailed c/o Rockpress Publishing, P.O. Box 99090 San Diego, CA 92169 USA.

NOTES

NOTES